D1151330

Succeed at psychometric testing

PRACTICE TESTS FOR
VERBAL
REASONING

INTERMEDIATE LEVEL

Simbo Nuga

HODDER
EDUCATION
OF HACHETTE LIVRE UK

New edition

Dedicated to

my husband and children

Julius, Benjamin and Julianne Nuga

The publisher has used its best endeavours to ensure that the URLs for external websites referred to in this book are correct and active at the time of going to press. However, the publisher and the author have no responsibility for the websites and can make no guarantee that a site will remain live or that the content will remain relevant, decent or appropriate.

Orders: please contact Bookpoint Ltd, 130 Milton Park, Abingdon, Oxon OX14 4SB. Telephone: (44) 01235 827720. Fax: (44) 01235 400454. Lines are open from 9.00–5.00, Monday to Saturday, with a 24-hour message answering service. You can also order through our website www.hoddereducation.co.uk.

British Library Cataloguing in Publication Data
A catalogue record for this title is available from the British Library.

ISBN: 978 0 340 96924 3

First Published 2004
Second edition 2008
Impression number   10 9 8 7 6 5 4 3 2 1
Year   2012 2011 2010 2009 2008

Copyright © 2004, 2008 Simbo Nuga

Typeset by Servis Filmsetting Ltd, Longsight, Manchester.
Printed in Great Britain for Hodder Education, part of Hachette Livre UK, 338 Euston Road, London NW1 3BH by Cox & Wyman Ltd, Reading, Berkshire.

Hachette Livre UK's policy is to use papers that are natural, renewable and recyclable products and made from wood grown in sustainable forests. The logging and manufacturing processes are expected to conform to the environmental regulations of the country of origin.

CONTENTS

FOREWORD

Should anyone tell you that a psychometric test will give an accurate indication of your level of intelligence, don't pay too much attention. It isn't necessarily true.

The credibility of the global psychometric testing industry rests on the belief of employers that a psychometric test will yield accurate and reliable data about a candidate's ability. Busy employers buy into the notion that a psychometric test will swiftly eliminate all the unsuitable candidates and deliver up only the best, brightest and most able candidates to the interview stage.

What is not widely known is that it is perfectly possibly for a candidate to drastically improve their own psychometric score by adopting a methodical approach to test preparation. The purpose of the *Succeed at Psychometric Testing* series is to provide you with the necessary tools for this purpose.

It is useful to know that a candidate's ability to perform well in a psychometric test is determined by a wide range of factors, aside from the difficulty of the questions in the test. External factors include the test environment and the professionalism of the test administrator; internal factors relate to the candidate's confidence level on the day, the amount of previous test practice the candidate has and the candidate's self-belief that they will succeed. While you cannot always control the external factors, you can manage many of the internal factors.

A common complaint from test takers is the lack of practice material available to them. The titles in the *Succeed at Psychometric Testing* series address this gap and the series is designed with you, the test taker in mind. The content focuses on practice and explanations rather than on the theory and science. The authors are all experienced test takers and understand the benefits of thorough test preparation. They have prepared the content with the test taker's priorities in mind. Research has shown us that test takers don't have much notice of their test, so they need lots of practice, right now, in an environment that simulates the real test as closely as possible.

In all the research for this series, I have met only one person who likes – or rather, doesn't mind – taking psychometric tests. You are not alone. This person is a highly successful and senior manager in the NHS and she has taken psychometric tests for many of the promotions for which she has applied. Her attitude to the process is sanguine: 'I have to do it, I can't get out of it and I want the promotion so I might as well get on with it.' She always does well. A positive mental attitude is absolutely crucial in preparing yourself for your upcoming test and will undoubtedly help you on the day. If you spend time practising beforehand and become familiar with the format of the test, you are already in charge of some of the factors that deter other candidates on the day.

It's worth bearing in mind that the skills you develop in test preparation will be useful to you in your everyday life and in your new job. For many people, test preparation is not the most joyful way to spend free time, but know that by doing so, you are not wasting your time.

The *Succeed at Psychometric Testing* series covers the whole spectrum of skills and tests presented by the major test publishers and will help you prepare for your numerical, verbal, logical, abstract and diagrammatic reasoning tests. The series now also includes a title on personality testing. This new title will help you understand the role that personality testing plays in both the recruitment process and explains how such tests can also help you to identify areas of work to which you, personally, are most suited. The structure of each title is designed to help you to mark your practice tests quickly and find an expert's explanation to the questions you have found difficult.

If you don't attain your best score at your first attempt, don't give up. Book yourself in to retake the test in a couple of months, go away and practise the tests again. Psychometric scores are not absolute and with practice, you can improve your score.

Good luck! Let us know how you get on.

Heidi Smith, Series Editor
educationenquiries@hodder.co.uk

Other titles in the series:

Critical Verbal Reasoning
Data Interpretation
Diagrammatic and Abstract Reasoning
National Police Selection Process
Numerical Reasoning Intermediate
Numerical Reasoning Advanced
Personality Testing
Verbal Reasoning Advanced

ACKNOWLEDGEMENTS

This book would not have been possible without the enthusiastic cooperation of Olu Ajayi, an Organisational Development Expert. Olu provided me with relevant and thoughtful materials and supported me throughout. I thank Jenni Williams, a Human Resources Specialist and Penny Hill, a Software Quality Expert, for freely providing ideas and advice and for checking and editing the initial manuscript.

Special thanks to the excellent team in the Maternity and Intensive Care Units at St Mary's Hospital in London for looking after my daughter and I. Sincere thanks to Bimbo Aridegbe, Uwamai and Doreen Igein, Grace Joseph, Dawn Watson, Jenni Williams, Olu Ajayi, Lily Wills, Mike and Catherine Shambler, Anna Morell, Kenan and Sam Maciel, John and Lizzie Davedas, Sarah Luke, Paul and Agathe Despois-Stalham, Chinwe Madubuike, Kemi Tob-Ogu, Pauline Le Bellec, Phillip and Irene Bremang, Herbert and Remi McCaulay, Joe and Patiwe Owusu, Peter and Ursula Collins, Rhoda Agerbak, Roger and Jackie Frimpong, Olurotimi Nuga, Titilope Nuga, Myriam Ba, Tokunbo and Yetunde Princewill, John Peart, Tony and Jennifer Westbrook, Ngozi Odigbo, Roch and Wende Miambanzila, Audrey Lofthouse, Yinka and Edna Adegbite, Happiness Brown, Nadine Poonawala, Lucy Joy, Esline Watson, Davinia Powell, Frank-Hector and Sylvie Yoba, James and Rita Akwetey, Vanessa Ince, Dephi and Bibi Longhi, Roger and Safie Mohila, John and Millie Akinlabi, Mr and Mrs Lanre Odunlami, Mrs Winnie Abdul-Malik, Sophie Okpala, Nisha McKinley, Gislain and Christian

Matingou, Abayomi Otubushin, Veronica Burgin, Lameen and Lili Abdul-Malik and to all our other friends who supported my family when I was critically ill in hospital. My heartfelt thanks to Tony and Gazey Umweni and Wayne and Jackie Scully for their extra special support during this difficult time. A big thank you to Mr Gbenga Osinowo and his family for the support and encouragement given to me over the years. I would like to express my gratitude to my parents Prince Christopher O. Otubushin and my mother Madam Esther O. Odufuwa for all their love, support and encouragement over the years. Without all of these people, this book would probably never have been completed.

Due thanks to Peter Rhodes for providing me with information on test providers. Thanks also to Roy Davis of Saville and Holdsworth for providing me with a few practice tests. I appreciate the willingness of Linda Murphy, Sue Avery and Paul McKeown of the Psychological Corporation to provide me with sample test materials.

Thanks are also due to SHL for Tests 1.12, 5.10 and 7.1–7.4; and to Civil Service Fast Stream Series (CSFSS) for Test 6.4.

CHAPTER ONE
INTRODUCTION

You can get it if you really want, . . .
But you must try, try and try, . . .
You'll succeed at last!

Yes, you can get it, get the job you are suited to do that is. The chorus of this well-known song by Desmond Dekker succinctly describes the message in this book. The words are very apt and do not mean that you have to try and fail several times – they simply mean practice makes perfect. It is very important to familiarise yourself with psychometric tests if you want to pass them. Practising questions significantly increases your chance of being able to get the job you desire if the recruitment process involves psychometric tests.

Employment and business opportunities advertised in the press or on the internet these days sometimes include benefits such as flexible working, foreign travel, long holidays, performance- and profit-related bonuses, shares, free or subsidised canteen, health insurance, training, free broadband with free internet telephone calls, rental accommodation, gym membership, life insurance, uniform, other job-related attire and great salaries to name a few. When most people see such advertisements they are initially quite excited until they find out that they have to take a test. At this point, some people choose not to apply or, if they have already applied and find out later during the selection process, they become less enthusiastic. Sometimes people have chosen to miss out on such life-enriching and career-enhancing opportunities because they have to take a psychometric test. The good news is that you don't have to miss out – you can succeed in psychometric testing.

In the competitive and unpredictable world we live in today it is important for us to take responsibility for the choices we make. We need to seize the opportunities presented to us and not allow challenges to stop us from realising our potential. One way of doing this is to equip ourselves with good communication skills. This skill becomes particularly relevant when we are presented with verbal reasoning tests. Organisations are now investing heavily in their screening process in their pursuit of business excellence. They know that they are only as successful as the quality of their employees. Businesses are placing increasing emphasis on an individual's competence in their aim to improve performance. Competencies such as interpersonal skills and various other personal qualities that are important to businesses can now be assessed using psychometric tests. The tests are usually developed by professional organisations who assess them for validity and reliability. These professional test developers sell tests to organisations and can also provide test administrative services. Psychometric testing is becoming widespread and many good jobs require an individual to take a test or a series of tests. It is essential that you banish any negative thoughts you have towards being tested in this way, so that you can concentrate on doing your best.

Psychometric testing is a standard and proven way of measuring an aspect of mental performance. Tests are used to assess verbal ability, explore personal attributes, such as personality and temperament, career or employment interests, values, attitudes and motivation. The tests include numerical reasoning, data interpretation, verbal reasoning and diagrammatic reasoning. The most commonly used types of psychometric tests are aptitude tests that concentrate on verbal reasoning and numeracy.

ABOUT THIS BOOK

This is a verbal reasoning practice book providing examples of tests, answers and explanations. Verbal reasoning questions come in different forms but they all rely on understanding the meaning of words and the structure of language. This book aims to explain the various formats in common use so that candidates can be better prepared for the test. It is often said that a test is only valid if it tests what it claims. A lot of effort has gone into choosing the tests in this book. There are just under 1550 questions in all, of which 1350 are brand new verbal reasoning tests designed to assess the candidate's aptitude in specific areas. Answers to and explanations of the tests are included. These tests are similar to those used in the recruitment, selection and appraisal process. The average length of the practice tests in this book could be longer than the average length of the verbal reasoning tests you will encounter in the real tests. This is to encourage you to work at a competitive pace. It is this knowledge that will give confidence in being able to successfully prepare and eventually pass verbal reasoning tests. The questions range in difficulty from the easy to the more challenging. The aim of this is to prepare you for the unexpected. Included in this book are a few practice questions from SHL. SHL is one of the most established and respected publishers of psychometric tests. The Psychological Corporation also gave permission for a few of their practice tests to be included in this book as examples.

This book aims to equip users by preparing them for verbal reasoning tests and helping them to develop personal awareness of attributes and skills. Those who will find this book useful include employers, jobseekers, recruitment specialists, junior to middle managers, people in supervisory roles such as personnel assistants, sales and customer service staff and management trainees, 'A' level students and people about to take tests for promotional reasons.

The book aims to be truly comprehensive and is divided into two main sections: Timed tests, and Answers to and explanations of timed tests.

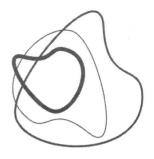

CHAPTER TWO
TIMED TESTS

There are three types of psychometric testing, these are: aptitude testing, ability testing and personality questionnaires. Ability tests focus on what the person is capable of achieving in the future or their potential to learn. Aptitude tests focus on your ability in a job. Professional test publishers such as SHL and the Psychological Corporation will use the job title to describe the test. There is a close relationship between the two types of tests because ability refers to general aptitude while aptitude refers to specific ability. This is to say that a general ability test might be made up of specific numerical, verbal and spatial ability scales produced as a test battery. These can then be marked and expressed as a specific measure of ability or aptitude, or together as a measure of ability.

Verbal reasoning tests measure your ability to understand and use words, interpret information, solve problems and make comparisons. Organisations place importance on verbal reasoning tests to assess the ability of a candidate to correctly express him/herself. It must be said that this is a basic but vital requirement in most jobs. The writing of contracts, promotional and marketing materials, critical memorandums and important correspondence to clients are possible tasks included in this requirement. It is also important for candidates to be able to express themselves properly on the telephone, as customer service is a vital element of any organisation's success.

There are various types of verbal reasoning tests to appraise a candidate's aptitude and capabilities. These include a variety of categories and approaches including vocabulary tests, verbal usage, grammar, sentence completion, verbal analogies, generic connections, verbal interpretation and critical reasoning.

In this chapter a section has been devoted to each of the major types of verbal reasoning tests. At the start of each section there is a brief description of the type of test followed by practice tests and hints on improving performance. This is a practice book so there is an answer box provided with each question. Simply write your answer in the box with a pencil so you can reuse the test. You could also choose to use a separate sheet of paper for this purpose.

Verbal reasoning tests are usually timed and generally multiple choice in format. The test writers make the test difficult and place tasking time constraints on the test taker. Simulate test conditions when doing the tests. Do them several times over if need be but reduce the time allocated with each attempt. Aim to be able to do eight questions in about three minutes or less. Take the time to learn the spelling and meaning of any word you are not familiar with or spell incorrectly. The list contains words that cause spelling problems for some people. The best way to excel is to have a good vocabulary and mastery of grammar and be familiar with taking tests.

There now follow various types of verbal reasoning tests.

1 VOCABULARY

This section aims to introduce you to a range of vocabulary tests. Vocabulary tests are simply spoken aptitude tests often used in appraising an employee's career development. It is essential in everyday life for a person to be able to communicate effectively. It is important to have solid knowledge of how to speak and write correctly because it is important for employees of an organisation to speak clearly when leaving answerphone messages, making enquiries, sending e-mails, writing memos, leaving notes for colleagues, writing reports, taking minutes of meetings, and writing contracts, to name a few tasks that would require the use of accurate spelling and appropriate use of words. Increasingly, employers and institutions want a standardised measurement to ensure that they recruit the right individuals in an increasingly competitive global environment. The most common vocabulary tests are questions on spelling.

The dictionary definition of the word 'vocabulary' is 'words that a person knows or all the words in a language'. The words used in these practice tests are those you should come across in everyday life and be aware of in a work environment. It is, however, difficult to prepare for these tests as a variety of areas such as politics, medicine, accountancy, law, current affairs, geography, economics, or suchlike could be drawn upon. You are advised to focus on increasing your vocabulary by reading newspapers, doing crosswords, playing word games, referring to a dictionary and a thesaurus.

You can also improve your vocabulary practically by having a notebook in which you write new words and their meaning. Learn the words that you intend to use and the context in which each must be used. Understand the use of the word in other parts of speech and learn the origins of words. Study the words daily and use them in writing and speaking. If you are not fluent in English you might decide to take classes, as this will provide you with a solid base on which to build your vocabulary.

The purpose of this section is not to teach you how to spell but to provide you with an opportunity to assess your ability to identify spelling mistakes. It is useful to own a good dictionary and to be aware of any inability to spell correctly. A person may find it difficult because of their level of fluency in English as a foreign language or because more specialist attention is required. The form of English language that is used throughout this book is 'standard English' as spoken in the United Kingdom.

There now follows the vocabulary practice tests. The first four tests consist of 40 questions each and you are required to identify the correct spelling of the word and write the letter corresponding to the correct spelling in the box. These words are chosen because they represent a fraction of words used socially and professionally. The aim is to provide you with a lot of practical exercises so that you are better prepared for such examinations. After the exercise you should ensure that you understand the meaning of all the words by referring to a dictionary. Below is a sample of the first type of vocabulary test.

SAMPLE QUESTION 1

What is the correct spelling of this word?

A	B	C	D
vaiens	veains	veins	veinns

C

The correct answer is veins, so write C in the box.

Vocabulary tests come in a few formats. Another way of assessing a candidate's spelling is to provide them with four different words and ask them to identify the word that has been spelt incorrectly by writing the corresponding letter in the box. Examples of these can be found in tests 1.5 to 1.8. These also consist of 40 questions each. There are in total over 1000 commonly used words that the reader may already know or learn to spell and understand. Emphasis has been placed on assessing these because words are the basis of any verbal communication.

SAMPLE QUESTION 2

Which of the following words is incorrectly spelt?

A dynamic
B consolidate
C prospectus
D Integrale

The correct answer is integrale, so write D in the box.

These tests can also be presented in the form of 'missing words' in a sentence. Sample question 3 illustrates this and test 1.9 provides you with an opportunity to familiarise yourself with this format. This format will also be used for the tests in the section on verbal application.

SAMPLE QUESTION 3

Choose the pairs of words that best completes each sentence.

François was not made ...... because he is ......

A	B	C	D	**B**
ridundant	redundant	redundancie	reddundancy	
multelingual	multilingual	moltilingual	multileingual	

The correctly spelt pair of words are redundant and multilingual so B is the answer to be written in the box.

Sometimes you will be presented with a list of about 50 to 100 words all correctly spelt and in alphabetical order and numbered. From this list about nine words will be chosen for each question. Some of the words in this group of nine are spelt incorrectly. Your task is to identify these words and write the corresponding number in the box provided. There may be up to four incorrectly spelt words. Sample test 4 is a good example of this format.

SAMPLE TEST 4

Below is a list of 20 correctly spelt words in alphabetical order. Below the list you will find a group of nine words. In this group there may be up to four spelling errors. You are expected to find the incorrectly spelt words and then locate them on the main list of words. Write the number corresponding to the word in the answer box.

List of 20 words

1 carrousel	11 seclusion
2 compassion	12 symposium
3 democratic	13 synergy
4 hibiscus	14 triplet
5 immaculate	15 ultramarine
6 neighbourhood	16 umbilical
7 nothingness	17 unapproachable
8 piety	18 waddle
9 politicking	19 wagonload
10 pristine	20 waistline

umbillical	triplet	piety
imaculate	carousel	symposium
unapproachable	hibiscus	neighbourhud

Answer

1	5	6	16

There are four incorrectly spelt words. The numbers have been written in the boxes provided.

SAMPLE TEST 5

Which of the following words form a word when spelt backwards?

A	B	C	D	E
paste	pans	page	pick	plenty

The answer is B. When 'pans' is spelt backwards we get 'snap'.

SAMPLE TEST 6

Write the letter of the one word which cannot be made from the letters of the word in capital letters.

INTERMEDIATE

A	B	C	D	E
made	term	make	date	media

The answer is C. The word 'intermediate' does not have a 'k'.

The answers and explanations to all the questions can be found in Chapter 3 of the book. It is now important to pause and think back to all you have read so far before proceeding to the tests. It is important to simulate an exam situation.

TEST 1.1 *(Answers on pages 179–180)*

What is the correct spelling for the following words? See how many you can do in 15 minutes.

	A	B	C	D	
1	association	asociasion	associasion	asociation	☐
2	archaeology	achiology	archiology	archeologie	☐
3	consolidetion	consolidation	consoledation	consolidasion	☐
4	bankrupcy	bankruptcie	bankruptcy	bankruptsy	☐
5	comprehensive	comprihencive	comprihensive	comprehenssive	☐
6	almanac	almernac	almanach	almernach	☐
7	astronot	astronaut	astraunot	astronut	☐
8	bucher	boutcher	butchar	butcher	☐

	A	**B**	**C**	**D**	
9	concurrent	concorent	concurent	koncurrent	☐
10	credibilitie	credibility	credibiliety	creadibility	☐
11	demonstraetive	demonstrative	demmonstrative	demonsstrative	☐
12	deadication	dedicaetion	dedicasion	dedication	☐
13	extraveganza	extravaganza	extravaganzer	extraveganzza	☐
14	cordial	cordeal	kordial	corddial	☐
15	konsecutive	consecutive	consercutive	consecittive	☐
16	fotography	photographie	photography	phottography	☐
17	demineralize	dimineralize	demeniralise	diminerralise	☐
18	hipopotamous	hippopotamus	hipopotemous	hepopotamous	☐
19	dicorous	decorus	decorious	decorous	☐
20	communitie	community	comunitie	cormunity	☐
21	carsette	casette	cassette	cassertte	☐
22	effieciency	eficiency	efficiency	effiensy	☐
23	wheid	weird	weeard	wheird	☐
24	digradable	degradable	degredable	degraddable	☐
25	conkuetish	coquettish	conquetish	conkuettish	☐
26	pheasant	feasant	phersant	pheazant	☐
27	meteorite	meateorite	miteorite	metteorite	☐
28	interweaving	intaweaving	interweving	interweeving	☐
29	encyclopedia	encyclopeadia	ensyclopeadia	encyclopedea	☐

	A	B	C	D	
30	demography	demografy	deamography	demographi	☐
31	allegator	aligator	alligetor	alligator	☐
32	parthetic	patethic	pattetic	pathetic	☐
33	quebble	quible	queble	quibble	☐
34	rationale	rartional	rasionale	rartional	☐
35	verterinarian	veterinarian	veteriranian	veterinnarian	☐
36	prefference	preference	preferrence	preferense	☐
37	equation	iquation	equeation	equasion	☐
38	dishonourable	deshonourable	dishornorable	dishonoureble	☐
39	relapse	relaps	relarpse	rellapse	☐
40	horoescopes	horroscopes	huroscopes	horoscopes	☐

TEST 1.2 *(Answers on pages 180–181)*

What is the correct spelling for the following words?
See how many you can do in 15 minutes.

	A	B	C	D	
1	dissappearance	disapearance	disappearance	disapperance	☐
2	programer	programmer	programar	programa	☐
3	inconvinience	inkonvenience	inconvenence	inconvenience	☐
4	entatainment	entertainment	enterteinment	enterttainment	☐
5	intigers	integers	integars	inntegers	☐
6	grause	grouse	grousse	grausse	☐

	A	**B**	**C**	**D**	
7	reprisentetive	reprezentative	representative	representetive	☐
8	inflehence	influennce	influense	influence	☐
9	enthologue	entholouge	enthoulogue	enthologe	☐
10	ferrensics	foerensics	forensics	forenssics	☐
11	perradigm	paradigm	paradiagm	parradigm	☐
12	naturallist	naturralist	naturaliste	naturalist	☐
13	purseuite	pursuit	purrsuite	poursuit	☐
14	guarentee	guarrantee	guarantee	guaranttee	☐
15	preddestined	pridestined	predesstined	predestined	☐
16	nourished	nourisshed	norished	knowrished	☐
17	kuriosity	curiosity	couriosity	courriossity	☐
18	arguments	argumments	aguments	argguments	☐
19	ellusive	ilusive	illusive	illusieve	☐
20	bezzare	biezzare	bizzare	bizarre	☐
21	ointment	oinntment	hointment	ointtment	☐
22	scandal	scandall	scanderl	scanddal	☐
23	fraggrance	fregrance	fragrance	fragranse	☐
24	modefication	mordification	modification	modifecation	☐
25	mysterie	mystery	mistery	misttery	☐
26	listtener	listiner	listener	listtenar	☐
27	adage	addage	adege	adagge	☐

	A	B	C	D	
28	confrontetion	confrontation	confrountation	confrontasion	☐
29	morrose	morose	morosse	moross	☐
30	hount	haunnt	huntt	haunt	☐
31	darision	dirision	derrission	derision	☐
32	frevolous	frivoulous	frivoulus	frivolous	☐
33	rutte	rute	ruote	route	☐
34	impatient	impateint	impetient	inpetient	☐
35	parraphrase	paraphrase	parafrase	parrafhrase	☐
36	flatery	flartery	flattery	flatterie	☐
37	anonymous	anonimous	anonymouse	anonymose	☐
38	hipnotise	hypnotyse	hypnotise	hipnotyse	☐
39	delebrately	delibraitely	deliberately	delebrattely	☐
40	arrogant	arroggant	aroggant	arrogernt	☐

TEST 1.3 *(Answers on pages 181–182)*

What is the correct spelling for the following words?
See how many you can do in 15 minutes.

	A	B	C	D	
1	konsistency	consistency	consestency	consistensy	☐
2	biterness	bitterness	bittaness	bitternes	☐
3	materialism	matirialism	mertirialism	materealism	☐
4	dentestry	dentistrie	dentisstry	dentistry	☐

	A	**B**	**C**	**D**	
5	exekutive	executeve	executtive	executive	☐
6	carbinet	cerbinnet	cabinett	cabinet	☐
7	insicurity	insecurerity	insecurity	insecurrity	☐
8	inffluenza	influenza	influhenza	influenzer	☐
9	neccesary	neserssary	necessary	necessarie	☐
10	tomorrow	tommorrow	tumorrow	tomorrowe	☐
11	plege	pledge	pledgge	pleddge	☐
12	descipline	discipline	disciplene	disciplin	☐
13	ellokuence	eloquence	helloquence	eloquennce	☐
14	dialema	dilemma	dilehmma	dilema	☐
15	imspectorate	inspectorate	inspecttorate	inspectoratte	☐
16	promenent	prominent	prominnent	promminent	☐
17	anouncement	announcement	announsement	announcemment	☐
18	commission	comission	commession	comision	☐
19	cene	scine	scenne	scene	☐
20	inntervension	intarvention	intervension	intervention	☐
21	consultetion	consultation	konsultation	consultasion	☐
22	proposale	propossal	proposal	proposall	☐
23	transparency	transperency	transparrency	transparensy	☐
24	obssolete	obsolette	obsolite	obsolete	☐
25	stratergy	strategy	strattegy	strategie	☐

	A	B	C	D	
26	chancellor	chanscellor	chancerlor	chancelor	☐
27	acessibility	accesibility	accessibility	accessebility	☐
28	phelanthropiste	pylanthropist	philanthropist	pylantropiste	☐
29	emphasis	enphasis	emphersis	emphasus	☐
30	elluminate	iluminate	illuminate	illumenate	☐
31	familiarlty	farmiliarity	farmelearity	familiarittie	☐
32	environnment	environment	envairment	envirronment	☐
33	ribelion	rebellion	rebelleon	reberllion	☐
34	phenommenon	phinomenon	phenomenone	phenomenon	☐
35	accelerating	acelerating	accelerrating	accellerating	☐
36	anteclimax	anteclaimax	anticlimax	anticlaimax	☐
37	caribbean	carribbean	caribbian	carribbian	☐
38	obssession	obsession	obsetion	urbsession	☐
39	appocryphal	apocryphal	apocriphal	apoccriphaal	☐
40	affluence	affluhence	affluense	affluennse	☐

TEST 1.4 *(Answers on pages 182–183)*

**What is the correct spelling for the following words?
See how many you can do in 15 minutes.**

	A	B	C	D	
1	mercinarys	mercenercies	mercinarys	mercenaries	☐
2	hespanic	hisphanic	hispanic	hesphanic	☐

	A	**B**	**C**	**D**	
3	harppening	happening	harpenning	harpening	☐
4	appraisal	apraisal	appreasal	appraissal	☐
5	performance	parfomance	performmance	performmance	☐
6	consoumer	konsumer	consumer	consumar	☐
7	portpholio	portfolio	portfollio	portfoleo	☐
8	shareholder	shearholder	shareholdar	sheaholder	☐
9	diarectorship	diarectourship	directorsheep	directorship	☐
10	bartery	battery	battry	batery	☐
11	incinnerate	insinerate	incinerate	insinerrate	☐
12	compoulsory	compulsery	compulsory	compulssory	☐
13	ocupation	occuppation	occupation	occupasion	☐
14	theraphy	teraphy	thearaphy	therapy	☐
15	hierarchy	highrachy	heirachy	heiracy	☐
16	coridor	corridor	coridour	couridor	☐
17	arseparagus	asparagus	asparragus	asparagose	☐
18	wenning	weening	weaning	wening	☐
19	trourser	trurser	trousser	trouser	☐
20	uniform	youniform	unifom	unifourm	☐
21	aticle	artticle	article	artecle	☐
22	parradox	paradox	perradox	paraddox	☐
23	legitimate	legetimate	lergitimate	legittimate	☐

	A	**B**	**C**	**D**	
24	supaficial	supperfecial	superficial	souperficial	☐
25	reharbilitate	rihabilitate	rehabelitate	rehabilitate	☐
26	fiscale	fisecale	fescale	fiscal	☐
27	stagering	stargering	stergering	staggering	☐
28	sueicide	suciade	suiside	suicide	☐
29	advertiselng	addvertising	advartising	advertising	☐
30	growtesque	grotesque	grotessque	groutesque	☐
31	extrecate	extricate	extrekate	extricaite	☐
32	greedlock	gridelock	gridlock	gridlocke	☐
33	wharffe	whafe	wharf	whaurfe	☐
34	ecentric	ekcentric	eccentric	exsentric	☐
35	ideilic	eyedelic	idylic	ideilic	☐
36	equity	equeity	ekuity	equitie	☐
37	dignitaries	dignetaries	deignitaries	digneitaries	☐
38	painstekingly	painsteakingly	peinstakingly	painstakingly	☐
39	prestige	presteide	presteidge	prestedge	☐
40	burowcracy	buereaucracy	bureaucracy	bureaucreacy	☐

TEST 1.5 *(Answers on pages 183–185)*

Which of the following words is incorrectly spelt?
You have 15 minutes to complete the questions.

	A	B	C	D	
1	psychology	consolidate	curryculum	behavioural	☐
2	convector	hazard	afixis	longevity	☐
3	albatrose	almanac	argument	quitting	☐
4	arears	assessment	assignment	subscribe	☐
5	bagpipes	bouming	barber	holistic	☐
6	convex	cornplaster	deeplete	merger	☐
7	despondent	detailled	dictaphone	olympic	☐
8	desociate	dividend	downturn	repugnance	☐
9	obliteration	eanestness	enclosure	application	☐
10	relic	especially	esperanto	perversse	☐
11	extermination	highlights	inspire	seieve	☐
12	puzzel	licentious	moderator	converter	☐
13	opportunity	surcharge	porkcupine	endowment	☐
14	prejudece	stimulate	prevalent	remortgage	☐
15	psychiatrist	recession	scamper	iridorlogist	☐
16	survey	swollen	technology	inflamation	☐
17	therapiste	verdict	workaholic	predisposition	☐

	A	**B**	**C**	**D**	
18	yawn	miscelaneous	naughtiest	aromatherapy	☐
19	blunder	calender	staples	specimen	☐
20	intenssive	organisation	answerphone	irritation	☐
21	receptionist	curtain	despensary	inherent	☐
22	manifestation	vehicle	viadoct	stubborn	☐
23	exercise	parentage	intermedeate	homeopathy	☐
24	bungalowe	accessory	chartered	interruption	☐
25	mediume	literature	authority	conventional	☐
26	milennium	superhighway	scrupulous	equivalent	☐
27	exhaustively	grasping	explanations	grueling	☐
28	equiped	straighten	twisted	stimulus	☐
29	absurd	substitutes	annoyarnces	ravage	☐
30	alcoholic	knowledge	narcolepsy	routin	☐
31	aliances	inefficient	mahogany	anaesthetic	☐
32	experiences	pesimistic	primarily	freelance	☐
33	contrary	profesor	perspective	innovative	☐
34	apathetic	bordensome	adversity	stammer	☐
35	investigation	museum	incompetent	suficiente	☐
36	quietness	integration	industrious	carbohidrate	☐
37	productive	exaggeration	parrasite	contingent	☐
38	constitutional	inevitable	fickleness	ossteopaty	☐

	A	B	C	D	
39	courtroom	magazine	imigrante	gymnasium	☐
40	parfunctoury	anarchy	exhibition	restaurant	☐

TEST 1.6 *(Answers on pages 185–187)*

**Which of the following words is incorrectly spelt?
See how many you can do in 15 minutes.**

	A	B	C	D	
1	successive	forgotten	futile	tranquile	☐
2	essayist	sorrowgate	appointments	prompt	☐
3	plucking	philosorpher	believe	exhilarating	☐
4	prescription	anihilation	cringing	boisterous	☐
5	misinterpret	ministerial	infalible	excruciating	☐
6	statuetory	reference	licence	slouch	☐
7	publishing	briefcase	flirtatious	agresive	☐
8	duvet	kinddagatten	apprenticeship	nervous	☐
9	flabagasted	categorically	prophylactic	pragmatism	☐
10	aggenda	relinquish	prospective	acquaintance	☐
11	detection	senility	insincere	cadeovascular	☐
12	establishment	comonwealth	tragedy	aerobics	☐
13	hypothetical	exagirate	hypocritical	refurbish	☐
14	neighbourhood	skeptecism	essential	disillusioned	☐

	A	**B**	**C**	**D**	
15	soliloquy	nightmare	paragraph	auxelearies	☐
16	ebb	stalk	experdetion	attitude	☐
17	onfastin	append	sprite	torrent	☐
18	compensation	parmitte	diminish	avalanche	☐
19	delve	nightfall	turnip	greggarious	☐
20	reviled	dicoy	rather	reclusive	☐
21	dether	oust	flavour	conceited	☐
22	squeze	rejuvenate	cede	solitary	☐
23	fiend	enrole	recoup	dismantle	☐
24	steer	ally	troupe	bewildar	☐
25	speculation	prerequisite	profesionalism	vandalism	☐
26	classics	examiner	midiocre	grudge	☐
27	acknowledge	whistle	autographs	ambasador	☐
28	elaborate	enomouse	desecration	protagonist	☐
29	dwindle	garbage	reinvegorate	villain	☐
30	inflicted	orthopaedic	disfunctional	soundtrack	☐
31	privilege	embarasing	punitive	cylindrical	☐
32	ludecrous	sanctuary	uniformity	rotund	☐
33	vengeance	propelled	sovreign	exquisite	☐
34	asault	exertion	counterbalance	montage	☐
35	nudist	landscape	affordeble	imminent	☐

	A	B	C	D	
36	oblivious	meringues	accustic	earthquake	☐
37	guitarist	tornedoes	scheme	stratospherically	☐
38	debilitating	typography	aftermath	satelite	☐
39	treadmill	velocity	queue	transmesion	☐
40	worldliness	allotment	imeasurable	millionaire	☐

TEST 1.7 *(Answers on pages 187–189)*

Which of the following words is incorrectly spelt?
See how many you can do in 15 minutes.

	A	B	C	D	
1	raspbery	smother	marinade	jockey	☐
2	spleen	parleamentary	metaphorically	mountaineering	☐
3	dislexic	federalism	multiplication	patriarchy	☐
4	porporting	enigmatic	seamstress	administrator	☐
5	fascistic	acrowbatic	stereotype	volunteer	☐
6	chauvenism	introverted	transmitted	archaeological	☐
7	opaque	dreary	effete	discepline	☐
8	retaliate	ironic	snipety	preponderant	☐
9	enthralled	misoginist	truculent	freighter	☐
10	taunt	thwarted	defiance	exercerbated	☐
11	torturous	domeneering	rhetorical	acrimonious	☐

	A	**B**	**C**	**D**	
12	raucous	claustropobic	retrospective	distort	☐
13	maverick	chandelier	swager	amicable	☐
14	tamarind	remeniscenes	psychoanalyst	denigrate	☐
15	acupuncture	ailment	sufragetes	anniversary	☐
16	nuroscientist	preposterous	synod	citation	☐
17	leniency	cowardiece	whimsy	peripheral	☐
18	phamaceuticale	favourite	boutique	indiscriminate	☐
19	pattern	subtraction	progression	alparbetical	☐
20	leopard	burdgeriger	exotic	assimilation	☐
21	european	toddler	squarre	symbol	☐
22	triangle	sequence	scouter	gram	☐
23	domestic	brarket	knight	brooch	☐
24	autum	tunic	semicolon	theorem	☐
25	restrictive	structureraly	socialism	clause	☐
26	phisical	municipality	obscure	courteous	☐
27	cathidrale	allegiance	draughtsman	fraternity	☐
28	heiress	automatic	omit	auxieliarie	☐
29	antecedent	illustration	vigore	hedge	☐
30	interrelate	yesterday	analogy	imiedeacy	☐
31	mechanical	vindecate	differ	century	☐
32	purchaser	brilliant	dexterrus	journalist	☐

	A	B	C	D	
33	proflliegate	cocktail	undertaker	anthem	☐
34	buzzard	adder	courtship	geolorgie	☐
35	phonetic	philharmonic	seegul	clutch	☐
36	teliparthy	zodiac	thermometer	topical	☐
37	ironmonger	narpekin	pavement	ladder	☐
38	underground	promescuos	advocate	archaic	☐
39	imaginative	scientist	shipwrecked	coasse	☐
40	serggent	mnemonic	repellent	tolerate	☐

TEST 1.8 *(Answers on pages 189–191)*

Which of the following words is incorrectly spelt? See how many you can do in 15 minutes.

	A	B	C	D	
1	astma	righteous	lottery	plethor	☐
2	consignment	parseword	weather	collaborator	☐
3	ultimatum	abrade	biscuit	leathar	☐
4	generalie	taxation	architecture	solo	☐
5	campaign	accommodate	discrepancy	atomique	☐
6	judiciary	freend	immigration	hatred	☐
7	autobiography	dervastetion	penicillin	hardship	☐
8	rethym	totalitarianism	ballot	brutal	☐

	A	B	C	D	
9	surveylance	niece	democracy	reshuffle	
10	parsimony	tattoo	curveacouse	concensus	
11	receipt	cholessterole	balcony	logical	
12	secretary	people	measure	tradeesionale	
13	furnace	foodstuff	recur	cryterion	
14	transistor	economic	desque	contradict	
15	parsuade	finance	nuclear	privacy	
16	alright	byologecal	clampdown	embryo	
17	ingenious	referendum	temporary	abartoire	
18	conveyancing	infringement	legacy	corregeusly	
19	apertitte	meticulous	chaos	formidable	
20	carterlogue	design	disguise	resources	
21	collection	fabric	chocolate	emberded	
22	gerafe	quack	antique	enhance	
23	derivative	graduate	distinguish	deesketes	
24	ingredients	decrease	chronolorgecal	multinational	
25	schedule	genuine	coalesion	villain	
26	foundation	idiosyncrasy	orgernism	hygiene	
27	fluoride	spreadsheet	terapiutic	editorial	
28	destructive	disability	inventories	aplerance	

	A	B	C	D	
29	combustion	ultrasound	diagnosis	cigarrettes	☐
30	microorganisms	varlves	underutilise	reliance	☐
31	metropolis	breeze	embroedered	nursery	☐
32	personnel	detours	rienergarse	multidirectional	☐
33	resiliency	procrastinate	jopardarsed	barriers	☐
34	gratuitous	accomplish	sparingly	elemenate	☐
35	scholarship	sixteen	copywriting	burdgetary	☐
36	econometric	mathematics	seelarnt	dimension	☐
37	proofreading	purnctuetion	merchandise	beverage	☐
38	reconcile	accountant	riplernish	conformance	☐
39	torbines	faculty	computerised	appropriate	☐
40	rifferrals	authors	laboratory	consultant	☐

TEST 1.9 *(Answers on pages 191–192)*

Choose the pair of words which best completes each sentence. See how many you can do in 10 minutes.

1 Shirley, the ...... has a ......

A	B	C	D	☐
herbalist	herberlist	herbaliste	herbbalist	
sponsor	spunsor	spunsore	sponsore	

2 ...... and ...... are terms used to describe positions of angles.

A	B	C	D	
paralel	parallel	paralleil	parallel	
adjarcent	adjacent	adjercent	adjasent	

3 Princess Camilla lookes quite ...... in the ...... dress.

A	B	C	D	
sophisticated	sofisticated	sophesticated	sophissticated	
jacquard	jackuard	jackard	jacqard	

4 Julius's new business has really ...... He has now ...... and property is now part of his portfolio.

A	B	C	D	
floorished	florished	flourished	flouriched	
dievasified	dyvassified	diversified	dyversified	

5 Tania, the ...... seeker needs a ......

A	B	C	D	
assylum	assylume	asylum	asyllume	
mastektomy	masstectomy	mastectomy	masttectomy	

6 The ...... is a ...... by profession.

A	B	C	D	
casanova	cassanova	cassanover	cassanorva	
cartographer	katograper	catografer	carthographer	

7 Drucilla is a ...... lady who knows how to make a tasty ......

A	B	C	D	☐
stuning	stunning	storning	stuneing	
sandewich	sandwich	sanndwitch	sandwhich	

8 The ...... who is also the account manager was able to close the lucrative deal so we celebrated with a bottle of ......

A	B	C	D	☐
technecian	tecknician	teknician	technician	
champegne	champaygne	champeyne	champagne	

9 The ...... shaped room has a newly ...... antique chair in the corner.

A	B	C	D	☐
trapizoid	trarpesoid	trapesoid	trapezoid	
opholstered	upholestered	upholsttered	upholstered	

10 She found out that she is ...... to dust since helping to carry the ......

A	B	C	D	☐
allegic	alergique	allergic	alleigic	
arteefacts	artifacts	artefacts	atefacts	

11 Sabrina saw her ...... on the lady when she was drinking from the ......

A	B	C	D	☐
whatch	watche	wartch	watch	
teombler	tombler	tummbla	tumbler	

12 The ...... complained about the level of ...... in the area.

A	B	C	D
leeseholder	leaseholder	lesseholder	leasseholder
trueancy	truancy	truehancy	truancey

13 The ...... confirmed that the victim was on her way to have ......

A	B	C	D
prousecutor	prosecutore	prosecutour	prosecutor
chemotheraphy	chimoutherapy	chemotheraphy	chemotherapy

14 The ...... expects ...... and comradeship from all.

A	B	C	D
bertallion	berttaleon	battalion	battaleon
excelence	excerlence	excellence	exsellence

15 The ...... caused by the ...... of the negotiation was understated.

A	B	C	D
inconvinience	inconveneence	inconvenience	inconnvenience
colapse	kolaspe	collapse	colasppe

16 The ...... manager ordered 60 kilos of ...... for use in their new recipe.

A	B	C	D
procurrement	procuorement	procurmment	procurement
coreander	corriander	coriandder	coriander

17 The project seems ...... but the plans need ......

A	**B**	**C**	**D**	
fiseble	feesible	feasible	feaseble	
rivision	revesion	revision	revission	

18 He enrolled at the ...... to study ...... art.

A	**B**	**C**	**D**	
university	unevercite	univarsity	univarcity	
dramatic	dramertic	drammatique	dramertic	

19 She looked ...... but took ...... to what the critic said about her.

A	**B**	**C**	**D**	
glamourous	glamorous	glamorrous	glamorus	
ofence	offence	offennce	offhence	

20 Jules found every task too ...... because she is ......

A	**B**	**C**	**D**	
tedious	tideious	tedeious	teddious	
anaemic	anemic	anaemick	anemick	

TEST 1.10 *(Answers on page 192)*

Here is a list of 100 correctly spelt words in alphabetical order. Below the list you will find 10 groups of nine words. In each group there may be up to four spelling errors. You are expected to find the incorrectly spelt words in each group and then locate them on the main list of words. Write the number corresponding to the word in the answer box.

See how many you can do in 5 minutes.

List of 100 words

1 alternative	29 blackout	57 dormouse
2 altogether	30 blockbuster	58 dualism
3 aluminium	31 bruiser	59 duffel
4 amalgamation	32 catapult	60 economical
5 ambassador	33 catarrh	61 efflorescence
6 ambidextrous	34 catastrophe	62 egyptology
7 ambience	35 cleavage	63 electronics
8 ameliorate	36 commencement	64 embankment
9 amenable	37 commendation	65 embassy
10 amnesty	38 commensurate	66 embroidery
11 amsterdam	39 commentary	67 farthermost
12 amusement	40 consequent	68 fascinate
13 anaesthesia	41 consideration	69 fastidious
14 analogy	42 consignment	70 filament
15 atmosphere	43 contagion	71 forfeit
16 attentive	44 contortionist	72 governance
17 auctioneer	45 convalescence	73 guatamala
18 audience	46 conventionality	74 guava
19 barometer	47 convergence	75 guesstimate
20 baroness	48 convulse	76 headquarters
21 bearing	49 demography	77 heterogeneous
22 because	50 demolish	78 holocaust
23 begrudge	51 demystify	79 homeopathy
24 bigamy	52 denominative	80 idiosyncrasy
25 biochemistry	53 descendant	81 illegitimate
26 bisect	54 destitute	82 imagination
27 blabber	55 discourteous	83 imbibe
28 blackcurrant	56 discretionary	84 impala

85 impartial
86 impediment
87 impregnable
88 impropriety
89 jollity
90 keepsake

91 legendary
92 legislative
93 misconception
94 neutron
95 nevertheless
96 oestrogen

97 parsley
98 pneumonia
99 sovereignty
100 surveillance

1

aluminium	dualism	amalgamation
contortionist	attentive	dermography
discendant	farthermost	convalescence

2

ambience	sovereignty	amusement
sorveillance	cleavage	commencement
facinate	bruiser	dimolish

3

discourteous	conventionality	commensurate
audience	destitute	alluminium
demystify	convulse	contagion

4

efflorescence	economical	discretionary
duffel	ambedextrous	neumonia
convergence	amalgamation	impregnable

5

ambience	ameliorate	auctioneer
hamsterdam	impartial	idosyncrasy
guatamala	baroness	altogerther

6

fastidious	embankment	fourfeit
bigamy	homeopathy	dormouse
guestimate	denominative	embroidery

7

auctioneer	barometer	impropriety
barroness	bearing	impala
governance	begrudge	embassy

8 begamy   ostrogen   consequent

neutron   keepsake   catarrh

jolity   egyptology   biochemistery

9 bisect   legendery   blackcurrent

misconception impediment blockbuster

electronics   blabber   catapult

10 cleavage   atmosphere   commendasion

consideration analogy   governance

consignment   anaesthesia alternative

TEST 1.11 *(Answers on pages 192–193)*

Here is a list of 100 correctly spelt words in alphabetical order. Below the list you will find 10 groups of nine words. In each group there may be up to four spelling errors. You are expected to find the incorrectly spelt words in each group and then locate them on the main list of words. Write the number corresponding to the word in the answer box.

See how many you can do in 5 minutes.

List of 100 words

1 abrasive	9 agamic	17 angularity
2 abscond	10 albatross	18 apache
3 abut	11 alfresco	19 badminton
4 accentuate	12 alibi	20 being
5 accessory	13 andes	21 bejewel
6 accomplice	14 android	22 belfry
7 accordion	15 anecdote	23 bellows
8 acetate	16 anguish	24 bequeath

25 besotted	51 compass	77 frost
26 binary	52 compassionate	78 ghastly
27 binge	53 compeer	79 glandular
28 binomial	54 daisywheel	80 glide
29 biotic	55 deferential	81 gloat
30 biro	56 defoliate	82 gradual
31 biscuit	57 defray	83 gurgle
32 bitters	58 defroster	84 gurkha
33 bizarre	59 densimeter	85 guru
34 borstal	60 disaffiliate	86 hanger
35 brittle	61 disrupt	87 ingenuity
36 broccoli	62 dissected	88 ingrain
37 bulwark	63 divine	89 inheritance
38 burnish	64 drizzle	90 initiator
39 bystander	65 drone	91 italic
40 byte	66 dynamite	92 numerology
41 byzantine	67 effloresce	93 nutrient
42 cheapskate	68 effrontery	94 officious
43 cheeseburger	69 egregious	95 oligopoly
44 cheesecloth	70 elementary	96 pantomine
45 chile	71 fatigue	97 pastorate
46 chinaware	72 february	98 pastrami
47 chippy	73 finial	99 penultimate
48 circulation	74 flutter	100 whistle
49 clearance	75 forceps	
50 cleat	76 forestation	

1 chile   biotique   frost
    abrasive   bizarre   bostale
    dissected   bitters   clearance

2 alibi   abscond   biro
forestetion   borstal   ghastly
binomial   andes   chinaware

3 abut   binge   biscuit
devine   forceps   drizzle
chippy   androide   accentuate

4 flutter   glandula   inheritance
broccoli   drone   aneckdote
accessory   binarie   circulation

5 disrupt   finial   glid
cleate   besotted   accomplice
anguish   dynamite   bulwalk

6 february   desafiliate   ingrain
gloat   bequeath   angularity
compass   burnish   accordion

7 fatigue   apache   gradual
bystander   byte   bellows
accetate   defroster   compassionate

8 badminton   elementary   ingenuity
gurggle   byzantine   belfry
compeir   densemeter   agamic

9 albatross   hanger   egregiouse
cheapskate   gurka   oligopoly
being   alfresco   daisiewheel

10 effrontery   cheeseburger   defoliate
ghuru   initiator   defray
deferential   bijewell   effloresce

TEST 1.12 (SHL PRACTICE TEST) *(Answers on page 193)*

Choose the pair of words which best completes each sentence. See how many you can do in three minutes. Write your answer in the box.

1 Now the company had the ...... to beat its main ......

A	B	C	D	E
opportunity	opportunity	opportounity	opportounity	None
competittor	competitor	competittor	competitor	of these

2 This ...... has given us many ...... for improving our product.

A	B	C	D	E
client	cliants	clients	cliants	None
suggestions	suggestions	sugestions	suggestions	of these

3 Results like these ...... on careful ......

A	B	C	D	E
dipend	dipend	dipends	dipends	None
implement-ation	impliment-ation	implement-ation	impliment-ation	of these

4 ...... the attack that had been made on him, his speech was ......

A	B	C	D	E
Considering	Considering	considering	considering	None
moderate	modarate	moderate	modarate	of these

5 The ...... letter included many elaborate ......

A	B	C	D	E
original	original	originel	originel	None
sentences	sentence	sentences	sentence	of these

6 I agree ...... your contention that the ...... should be favourably considered.

A	B	C	D	E
with	with	to	to	None
aplication	application	aplication	application	of these

7 Costs are to be ...... by ......

A	B	C	D	E
repayed	repayed	repaid	repaid	None
instalmants	instalments	instalmants	instalments	of these

8 The ...... is ...... if you do not pay the premium on time.

A	B	C	D	E
policy	pollicy	polisy	polisy	None
forfieted	forfeated	forfieted	forfeated	of these

TEST 1.13 *(Answers on page 193)*

Which of the following form words when spelt backwards? Write your answer in the box provided. See how many you can do in 3 minutes.

	A	B	C	D	E
1	mark	mist	moor	mock	must
2	stressed	steam	seeds	sower	smoke
3	test	kick	cash	trap	kite
4	words	wolf	paper	pack	french
5	bible	praise	catch	direct	paws
6	emit	zone	lane	roads	purse

	A	B	C	D	E	
7	design	learn	direct	laid	fun	☐
8	result	loot	notice	your	vision	☐
9	style	frame	health	sight	stop	☐
10	offer	regard	rats	help	stock	☐
11	draw	issue	next	find	often	☐
12	hectic	ocean	deal	make	early	☐

TEST 1.14 *(Answers on page 193)*

Write the letter of the one word which cannot be made from the letters of the word in capital letters in the box. See how many you can do in 5 minutes.

	A	B	C	D	E	
1 PAINTER	rain	print	tramp	nape	trip	☐
2 COUNTRY	cope	you	count	out	try	☐
3 ELEPHANT	plant	tap	leap	paint	ant	☐
4 WEATHER	wear	weak	tear	earth	there	☐
5 VEGETABLE	get	cest	able	age	table	☐
6 STATIONERY	tyres	noisy	stone	nation	ration	☐
7 PETROL	role	rope	roe	rate	pet	☐
8 GENERAL	large	rage	gear	ear	lake	☐
9 TRANSPORT	port	ran	train	sport	tap	☐
10 RESTAURANT	rest	ant	test	tan	tape	☐

		A	B	C	D	E	
11	DELIVER	liver	ever	ear	live	eve	☐
12	SENTENCE	ten	stop	tense	sent	scene	☐
13	DETAINS	instead	neat	dear	site	staid	☐
14	DANCE	ace	cone	can	den	and	☐
15	ESCAPE	cap	pace	cape	ape	cope	☐
16	COURAGE	age	cage	cane	rage	our	☐
17	LISTENED	list	lease	end	need	ten	☐
18	TERRACE	race	crate	car	trace	erase	☐
19	EXPENSIVE	pen	spent	sieve	expense	eve	☐
20	DISTANT	stain	ants	dint	step	stand	☐

2 VERBAL USAGE

It takes discipline and effort to communicate effectively. If you cannot do this you will find that it leads to misunderstanding and can even affect your career prospects. It is therefore beneficial to improve your communication and interpersonal skills. Some verbal reasoning tests include the use of words that sound the same or similar, but have different meanings. In the English language these words can be termed ambiguities. There are also words that can be confused with other words, and these are termed confusable words. It is necessary to be aware of them and to use them correctly. You should refer to a dictionary in order to understand the differences between them and try making up phrases, sentences and questions of your own in order to increase your confidence with their usage.

AMBIGUITIES

Examples of words that fall into this category are:

Effect	Affect	Wave	Waive
Ascent	Assent	Right	Write
Brake	Break	Sent	Scent
Brooch	Broach	Peek	Peak
Cut	Caught	Mourning	Morning
Waste	Waist		

Refer to a dictionary if you need to confirm your knowledge of their meaning.

Illustrated below is an example of the format used to test a person's knowledge of such words.

SAMPLE TEST 1

Write down the word that sounds the same or similar to the word you have been given but is spelt differently.

1   weather   ___*whether*___

Whether is the word similar to weather in pronunciation.

SAMPLE TEST 2

Place the correct word into the gaps in the sentences below:

1   The guiding ...... is self-denial.

principal	principle

The missing word is 'principle', which means 'moral rule guiding behaviour'. Principal is the word used to describe the head of a school.

CONFUSABLE WORDS

Some words are similar in meaning or they simply look or sound alike so people use them interchangeably but incorrectly. Listed below are examples of confusable words. Use a dictionary to check that you know their correct meaning and try to make up sentences of your own.

historic	historical	irritable	nervous
beaches	coast; shore	gentle	polite
much	many	dependent	dependant

sympathetic	friendly	ashamed	embarrassed
journey	voyage; trip	anniversary	birthday
rent	hire	discussion	quarrel
spend/t	pass/ed	customs	habits
less	fewer		

Below is a sample of a test on confusable words.

SAMPLE TEST 3

Complete the passages below by choosing the correct word from the set.

1   Many ...... have been going to Kenya for their holidays.

strangers	foreigners	aliens

The correct answer is 'foreigners'. One could be a stranger in a place or something could be alien to someone but foreigners go on holidays to other countries.

SAMPLE TEST 4

If the word CAGE is written in code, it will look like this: %&£@

Now write the word AGE using the code.

The answer: is &£@

Now attempt the following exercises. Please read the instructions carefully before proceeding.

TEST 2.1 *(Answers on page 194)*

Write down the word that sounds the same or similar to the word you have been given but is spelt differently. See how many you can do in 20 minutes.

1 his	_____	**16** red	_____
2 byte	_____	**17** be	_____
3 herd	_____	**18** hare	_____
4 site	_____	**19** worked	_____
5 fore	_____	**20** meat	_____
6 stationary	_____	**21** course	_____
7 counsel	_____	**22** boar	_____
8 grate	_____	**23** here	_____
9 cheque	_____	**24** of	_____
10 allowed	_____	**25** bye	_____
11 flour	_____	**26** grip	_____
12 seat	_____	**27** two	_____
13 need	_____	**28** sun	_____
14 knew	_____	**29** extant	_____
15 sock	_____	**30** bore	_____

31 fate	_____	**36** key	_____
32 rest	_____	**37** knit	_____
33 ring	_____	**38** ale	_____
34 or	_____	**39** naval	_____
35 pull	_____	**40** rap	_____

TEST 2.2 *(Answers on pages 194–195)*

Place the correct word into the gaps in the sentences below. See how many you can do in 10 minutes.

1 The proprietor wrote the first draft of the contract on a ...... of paper.

peace	piece

2 You need the password to ...... the database.

excess	access

3 Timothy wanted to buy and ...... the newspaper.

read	rid

4 The chairman ...... the proposal by courier.

sent	scent

5 The textile designer uses a lot of ...... on a daily basis.

die	dye

6 She was not able to produce the report ...... to a systems failure.

due	dew

7 The ...... disposal van comes every week.

waste	waist

8 Tanya received the message delivered by the ...... horologist.

mail	male

9 It does not ...... a lot in the Sahara.

rain	reign

10 ...... ancestors lived in Serbia.

their	there

11 The town is very ...... with tourists.

popular	populous

12 Does the river Danube have a ...... ?

dam	damn

13 Benjamin speaks with a Canadian ......

accent	assent

14 The mountaineer aims to reach the ...... of the mountain in five days.

peek	peak

15 The angler ...... a twenty-pound trout.

cut	caught

16 The little shy boy is allergic to ...... products.

dairy	diary

17 The lawyer encouraged his client to ...... her right to appeal.

waive	wave

18 It is important to exercise your ...... to vote.

right	write

19 She had a very intricate ...... on her jacket.

brooch	broach

20 The negative publicity will adversely ...... his marriage.

effect	affect

21 The surgeon noticed ...... arteries during the procedure.

tree	three

22 All the employees can request a season ...... for travel purposes.

lone	loan

23 The widower has been in ...... for over a year.

morning	mourning

24 The shop assistant usually has a siesta during her lunch ......

brake	break

TEST 2.3 (Answers on page 195)

Place the correct word into the gaps in the sentences below. See how many you can do in 15 minutes.

1 Kingsley has ...... for that company for 20 years but he has now chosen to be self-employed.

walked	worked

2 Michael ...... me to use his personal computer.

aloud	allowed

3 I will be leaving the Seychelles on Saturday so I will ...... with you in less than a day.

bee	be

4 I have to perm my ...... regularly.

hair	hare

5 I ...... the answer to the question but I was simply not prepared for this particular exercise.

knew	new

6 I ...... that Marcia has had her operation.

herd	heard

7 That child looks small in stature but she has a strong ......

grip	gripe

8 Ainsley took a taxi from ...... to his destination.

here	hear

9 He is such a ...... friend to Ian and Sally.

great	grate

10 I need to add some ...... to the shredded carrots when making the cake.

flour	flower

11 Kate will be having her hair ...... for the first time in 20 years, tonight.

caught	cut

12 You will find all you need in ...... bag.

his	hiss

13 The local ...... is in charge of law and order.

council	counsel

14 Chloe finds that sponge too ...... because she has very sensitive skin.

coarse	course

15 She has eaten ...... much and I hope she will not fall ill.

too	two

16 It is sometimes easier to take a ...... and watch.

sit	seat

17 I paid for my shopping by ...... yesterday.

check	cheque

18 Be careful of the dog, it can ...... you.

bite	byte

19 The outfit I bought for the wedding is made ...... chiffon.

off	of

20 Joshua will ...... some money to take with him on holiday.

knead	need

21 I love eating ...... so I will find it hard to be a vegetarian.

meat	meet

22 Jennifer has found one ...... but she now has to look for the other.

suck	sock

23 That car has been ...... for well over a year.

stationery	stationary

24 The ...... manager would like us to have a meeting.

sight	site

25 Jatinder, the farmer, has put the wild ...... in a cage.

bore	boar

26 Kojo, the son of the diplomat, has a ...... coat.

red	read

27 Sally has been waiting for well over a month for your proposal, can you ensure that she receives it ...... this time next week.

by	bye

28 Hello Craig, I left my mobile phone on your table. Can I come to ...... it up tonight?

peak	pick

29 Bethany will be going to see the doctor on Friday because she found a lump on her ......

cheek	chick

30 If you want to make a pledge for charitable purposes, you may choose to sign a ...... of covenant.

did	deed

TEST 2.4 *(Answers on page 195)*

Complete the passages below by choosing the correct word for each set. See how many you can do in 10 minutes.

1 A lot of tourists go to visit the ...... monuments in Greece.

historic	historical

2 Gislaine loves the sandy ...... and the hot tropical sun.

beaches	coast	shore

3 ...... people go to the capital of Gambia without going to the surrounding villages.

much	many

4 The monks seem very ...... and hospitable to their guests.

sympathetic	friendly

5 Whilst in Egypt, Grace took a boat ...... on the river Nile.

journey	voyage	trip

6 Amanda ...... a bike and visited some archaeological sites in Prague.

rented	hired

7 She ...... a week at a cookery school in Switzerland.

spent	passed

8 A Mini consumes ...... petrol that a Jeep.

less	fewer

9 Aisha was extremely ...... before and during the audition.

irritable	nervous

10 Titilope was very ...... and thanked me for the the meal.

gentle	polite

11 A lot of people in the third world look after their ...... elderly relatives.

dependent	dependant

12 The politician who is now married to the rich man used to feel ...... of her humble origins.

ashamed	embarrassed

13 We always go to a restaurant to celebrate our son's ......

anniversary	birthday

14 The executives of the two companies had a productive ...... about the takeover.

discussion	quarrel

15 It is essential for Thierry to understand the ...... and religious beliefs of his adoptive parents.

customs	habits

16 It is essential for us to be more ...... to the needs of the elderly.

sensitive	sensible

17 She has become quite insecure since she failed her test and has become quite ...... to critical remarks

sensitive	sensible

18 George is very responsible and organised for his age. He is just quite simply very ......

sensitive	sensible

19 The wound from his operation will take time to ......

cure	heal	treat

20 The athlete tested positive for the banned ......

stimulus	stimulant

21 It is now widely accepted that the Harry Potter books serve as a ...... and encourage children to read more.

stimulus	stimulant

22 His flu had to be ...... with antibiotics.

cured	healed	treated

23 He was ...... only after they had used various herbal remedies.

cured	healed	treated

24 That medicine is a ...... because after taking it you can stay awake and get things done even if you are tired.

stimulus	stimulant

TEST 2.5 (Answers on page 196)

If in a code the word 'HOSPITAL' is written as shown below, write the following words using the code in the space provided. See how many you can do in 5 minutes.

H	O	S	P	I	T	A	L
+	&	×	%	@	$	?	\

1 SHOP _____

2 POST _____

3 SOIL _____

4 SPOT _____

5 PAL _____

6 HOP _____

7 SPIT _____

8 SLOP _____

9 TIP _____

10 HOT _____

11 LAP _____

12 SALT _____

13 LIP _____

14 HIT _____

15 PIT _____

16 SAIL _____

17 STOP _____

18 TAIL _____

19 SOAP _____

20 SLIP _____

21 TOP _____

22 HAT _____

23 POT _____

24 HOST _____

25 SPOIL _____

26 HOIST _____

27 SLIT _____

28 HIP _____

29 SLOT _____

30 SIP _____

3 VERBAL APPLICATION

The sentence is the basic unit of communication and words, phrases and clauses are elements of communication. The function of a sentence is to communicate facts, emotions and various issues with clarity, exactness, correctness and economy no matter how difficult.

It is important for an employer to have confidence in an employee's ability to communicate effectively. Some of the issues that would be considered during a recruitment and selection process are the ability to appropriately and consistently address an audience or deal with a subject matter. How well a person speaks and writes depends on their mastery of grammar and vocabulary. This section focuses on how grammar is tested.

Verbal application tests assess a person's understanding of the principles of grammar. It tests aspects of fluency, language accuracy, pronunciation and interactive communication. Candidates are expected to understand grammatical concepts and rules. It is essential for you to know the parts of speech and their various kinds, some of which are illustrated below:

The parts of speech	Kinds of:
The noun	Common and Proper, Concrete and Abstract, Collective, Inflection, Number, Gender and Personification
The pronoun	Personal, Demonstrative, Indefinite, Relative, Interrogative, Numerical, Reflective and Intensive and Reciprocal
The verb	Transitive and Intransitive, Auxiliary, Strong and Weak, Regular and Irregular, Conjugation, Person, Number, Tense, Mood
	Voice – Active, Passive, Progressive and Emphatic forms

The parts of speech	Kinds of:
The adjective	Descriptive, Common, Proper, Limiting, Articles and Pronominal
The adverb	Simple, Conjunctive
The conjunction	Coordinating, Subordinating
The preposition	Object, position and meaning of preposition
The interjection	Expression of emotions

The aim of this book is not to teach grammar. For those who regard this as a weakness you can choose to study English by distance learning, part-time or full-time study. You can also memorise some of these concepts in order to improve your performance in the test.

Grammar is tested either through error identification or sentence completion. Test sentences have spaces and you need to find the appropriate word to occupy these spaces. The spaces may come in pairs, you have to identify the correct pair to complete the sentence.

SAMPLE QUESTIONS

1 ERROR IDENTIFICATION

  1 Which of the following sentences is grammatically correct?

    a The young girl snatched the book off of me.

    b Sally should have took the bags to the reception.

    c The horse was very enormous.

    d The shirt is brilliant white in colour.

Answer and explanation

It is important for you to understand some principles of English grammar. There are errors in (a) to (c). In (a) the word 'of' is not required and in (b) the correct word is 'taken' and not 'took'. In (c) the word 'very' is not needed as the word 'enormous' means 'very large'. The grammatically correct answer is (d).

2 SENTENCE COMPLETION

The idea is for you to identify the best possible word/s to complete the sentence.

1 Kate likes using custard when making desserts. She uses a special brand because of the taste and she reckons that the name is ...... with good quality.

   a similar

   b linked

   c connected

   d synonymous

Answer

The objective is to identify the best possible word and in this case it is 'synonymous', which means 'closely associated'. The correct answer is therefore (d).

There now follows some tests.

TEST 3.1 *(Answers on page 197)*

Identify the best possible word to complete the sentence. Write your answer in the box. See how many you can do in 12 minutes.

1 Ahmed is a strange man, I like him but he is very ......

    a pretentious   **c** phoney

    b hypocrite   **d** untrue

2 Jean-Paul likes to be different but his behaviour can sometimes be ......

    a annoying   **c** balanced

    b distraction   **d** typical

3 The curriculum vitae of the ...... is very detailed.

    a applicant   **c** students

    b graduates   **d** pupils

4 A terrible social ...... grips Dawn because of gaps in her knowledge.

    a paralysis   **c** helplessness

    b conquest   **d** indifference

5 Tony and Julius went into ...... and they work well together.

    a task   **c** partnership

    b company   **d** agreement

6 The breakdown in diplomatic talks meant that military intervention was ......

   a agreed   **c** happening

   b strength   **d** inevitable

7 The company went into ...... because of bad financial management.

   a bankrupt   **c** receivership

   b loss   **d** adverse

8 James has ...... a lot this year because he is more organised.

   a completion   **c** floated

   b harden   **d** accomplished

9 Veronica is quite ...... and humble at the same time.

   a obvious   **c** disturbance

   b expressive   **d** capacity

10 The bodyguard was mistakenly ...... with stones.

   a pelted   **c** bothered

   b thrown   **d** armed

11 Norman was ...... for not sending his children to school.

   a found   **c** criticised

   b encouraged   **d** concern

12 The information gathered from the suspect is full of ......

  a dispute   **c** opulence

  b contradiction   **d** contentment   ☐

13 The auditor made a ...... in his report.

  a suggest   **c** thought

  b recommendation   **d** wishful   ☐

14 George has been ...... to meditate on a daily basis.

  a encouraged   **c** assurance

  b bent   **d** ask   ☐

15 Pamela dislikes taking the train because she suffers from ......

  a distasteful   **c** disjointed

  b claustrophobia   **d** chuckled   ☐

16 Thank you for coming to see Polly in hospital, but you ...... have done it.

  a needn't   **c** wouldn't

  b couldn't   **d** might   ☐

17 Marilyn finds Tarik too ...... for his own good.

  a self-assured   **c** perfectionist

  b selfishness   **d** arrogance   ☐

18 You need money and commercial skills to build a ...... business.

a tasking   **c** shine

b successful   **d** helpful ☐

19 Charlie was rather ...... by the allegations.

a terrific   **c** perplexed

b affect   **d** experienced ☐

20 Prity Patel was completely ...... about going to America.

a checked   **c** fabulous

b unenthusiastic   **d** capacity ☐

21 Charlotte was ...... exhausted after her shift at work.

a calm   **c** nervous

b utterly   **d** whole ☐

22 Passing the driving test for some people is quite an ......

a hope   **c** achievement

b show   **d** ability ☐

23 Hitesh was ...... about his parent's choice of bride.

a effected   **c** flabbergast

b humour   **d** happy ☐

24 Titilope is not only pretty, she is also ......

a poor   **c** photogenic

b comic   **d** servant ☐

TEST 3.2 *(Answers on page 197)*

Which of the following sentences is grammatically correct? Write the letter corresponding to the correct answer in the box provided. See how many you can do in 15 minutes.

1 **a** I would have come sooner if I known you was here.

    b Lily approves of what her daughter does.

    c If the sentence had gotten the correct spacing, it would be complete.

    d The cake could have been burned black.

2 **a** Maises mother would have understood knowing what to do if she was alive.

    b Tony had learnt a lot of english language since arriving to this country.

    c Write a short report and hand it to Jean-Luc in the morning.

    d Mary had gotten hold of the job in the bank 3 years ago.

3 **a** We've always wrote your name clearly before now.

    b Benjamin told Esther that Skiing is a dangerous sport.

    c The furniture that was bought wasn't even what I ordered.

    d The student are starved and hungry and the canteen is next door.

4 **a** The Foreign secretary is waiting for some significantly important information.

   b I've always drank a little good wine with my meals.

   c I was pleasantly pleased to find the picture painting by Leonardo.

   d Chloe is interested in learning to become a parachutist.

5 **a** Myriam passed her driving test first time, surprising everyone.

   b A spanking brand new video shop has opened up in Keswick Gardens.

   c Simon's wife has a terribly violent headache.

   d There is many old, aged towns and villages in the countryside.

6 **a** All handbags looks practical and attractive, to the viewer or onlooker.

   b The local Garden Center employs over 15 people locally.

   c Wayne gave Tara a ring as soon as he arrived.

   d There are 16 much-loved stories told in the very popular, much loved story book.

7 **a** Luxurious showers were build into the Caravan's bathroom area.

   b I feel as if my heads on fire.

   c Akosua gave birth to a very beautiful girl.

   d I'm sure the Librarian will remember I return the book last week.

8 **a** Angel recently became a grandmother.

    b You must have miss your train.

    c The VIP are to fly into Europe tomorrow.

    d She asked why we come so early. ☐

9 **a** Shelly ask what happen to her Chocolates.

    b The council meet next Tuesday.

    c Jean look as if he can do with a stiff drink.

    d Gabriel fell off his bike. ☐

10 **a** Where you go for your holidays last summer?

    b The constable was watchfully keeping a eye on things.

    c He slept peacefully on the convertible bed.

    d They fell for love ten years ago. ☐

11 **a** Some people never see snow before.

    b While he was shopping, they broke into his car and stole £100.

    c The play wasn't really worth reviewed scrutiny.

    d Tariq ask Diane to come see a film with him tonight. ☐

12 **a** Our class start in French next week.

    b Mrs Khan didn't have to have her hair combed yesterday.

    c Can you picture a image of a green & purple tie.

    d If people drove more carefully, there would be fewer accidents. ☐

13 **a** It is not right to read other people's letters.

    b It's high time you have a hair cut.

    c Eric is in serious difficulty finding his way out.

    d The fire done seriously spread to the next building.

14 **a** Could you lent me your text book.

    b Thankfully it was a quiet night tonight.

    c Sophie's pile of work has been finished off.

    d Mrs Chan bought a new coat last week.

15 **a** The dishwasher looks a little bit too dangerous to me.

    b The electrician will be probably coming round tomorrow.

    c Sade phoned several other people on my instruction.

    d They go home after finishing off on their job.

16 **a** I'm not sure if he and his wife will certainly be in.

    b It is important for you to keep your credit card in a safe place.

    c Luca, the accountant is getting a bit of difficulty with putting a bill payment through.

    d She looks at his body piercing and was surprise that he had had it done.

17
  a Cathy promised them that Jo should be confirm.

  b They took the notice off the wall.

  c Olive does meet very interesting people at her place of work.

  d People often mistaken her for her sister.

18
  a Your chldren like cartoon films, don't they?

  b I got no news since Thursday evening.

  c Her weekend was enjoyable and superior.

  d Did you know she hasn't gotten anything to wear tonight.

19
  a I'm afraid I haven't the spare moment in time to do it.

  b Timothy didn't have any other things to say.

  c He's supposed to meet me here now.

  d Bejamin is a conscientious individual. Don't you think?

20
  a I got the Garage to sort it.

  b Marco used a mnemonic device to memorise his speech.

  c Deigo was following up on them investments.

  d We added up the plenty money.

21 **a** My mum said them people can't talk to me like that.

  b Rotimi's father is very proud of his son's achievement.

  c Your friends idea is worth a thorough going in to.

  d The government don't give me many assistance, only a little money weekly. ☐

22 **a** Miguel disapproves of lap dancing because of his religious belief.

  b We hear that a fire broke out in your house.

  c She saying that he was injured by the mob.

  d Please can you scribble a note for them for me sake. ☐

23 **a** Nelly, the nutritionist is from a small village in France.

  b Them attempted going home alone.

  c It's you she talking to.

  d It is enormously very difficult to understand the lecturer. ☐

24 **a** The rent isn't all that.

  b The delivery done made in the nick of time.

  c Jean-Luc has watched the video about Stuart Little's life several times.

  d The data was collectively gathered by all of us. ☐

25 **a** The question asked was most extremely profound.

b Jason said that him would come out to play soon.

c Where did I pack my makeup.

d Will Annick be going abroad for her honeymoon? ☐

26 **a** Listen to me carefully and this won't take long to explain.

b Gislaine got her first job by the employment agency.

c First go empty the dustbin and then put the gloves on back.

d Sally was puzzled by the news, but there was no time to panic. ☐

27 **a** The patient thinks that Dr Coker is extremely understanding and resourceful.

b Keiran took the tape recorder of off the electrician.

c The impressionist painting is very ginormous in size.

d Ship building is an extremely challenging herculean project. ☐

28 **a** Dorothea is a very thorough conscientious nurse.

b Yusuf is a part qualified accountant. He is hardworking but he does not socialise.

c The project is legally legitimate but it requires a good planner to execute it.

d You need to be stylishly vogue and fashionable for the occasion. ☐

29 **a** Paula Cheng is a studious bookworm on the course.

  b Ian is a reliably loyal and truthful friend.

  c Tyron showed a lot of restraint in staying calm during that confrontation.

  d The hypnotist is substantially, quite importantly messing with her mental state.

30 **a** Ms Lindstrom is irate deeply angry with the way she has been treated today.

  b Georgiou needs essential oils in his bath to totally, fully completely be relaxed.

  c Elisabeth is so unspoilt innocent and her qualities are so rare these days.

  d Lili Wong is looking so fit and well. She has been going to the gym regularly.

TEST 3.3 *(Answers on page 198)*

Which of the following sentences is grammatically incorrect? Write the letter corresponding to the correct answer in the box provided. See how many you can do in 15 minutes.

1 **a** The caller hung up before I got to the phone.

  b Do let me know how sweet you like your tea.

  c Charlene's flight left London at 6.30 a.m.

  d Andrew's stubborness and pride lead to downfall.

2 **a** How long have you been working as a nurse?

b Jenny is a great fan of the musician who is now famous.

c Lydia met her husband in Venice.

d Hassan's family are refugee in Dublin.

3 **a** Tegan forgot to bring the wedding rings with him. He is so forgetful and disorganised.

b The flight itself was smooth enough; what I found terrifying was the clown who sat next to me.

c The man who act like a clown is a drunk.

d There will be fun for the whole family including free seminars on parenting.

4 **a** I understood that refunds will be given in any circumstance.

b The idea to grant new rights to British workers is contained in the proposals for rewriting the EU constitution.

c What will you have been doing in five years time?

d The journalist reported from the middle of the war zone.

5 **a** We offer a wide range of accredited courses specifically for disabled students and students with learning difficulties.

b That Gameshow give fantastic prizes.

c Charles was lucky to survive after falling down a 100ft cliff.

d A dangerous paedophile was jailed for only three years.

6 **a** Hazel will visit Jordan, Egypt and Israel as part of a gruelling six day international tour.

b Beatrice went to the box office and bought a ticket for next Monday's show.

c Esther has a new job. Her first day in it will be the 20th of October.

d At some stage, I hear a loud noise from the auditorium.

7 **a** The marathon runner has taken seven hours to finish.

b A bird flew into the room during our French lesson.

c A friend of mine rang when I was watching a very interesting television programme.

d Shall we go to the museum on our day off?

8 **a** I'd like Thierry to hurry so that we do not miss our train.

    b Mr DeSilva buys the *Guardian* newspaper on a daily basis because he finds it interesting.

    c Community spirit don't exist here no more.

    d Sebastian, the athlete turned politican is considering acting in a film.

9 **a** If you want help choosing a course ask to speak to the Information and Advice Officer.

    b Her husband went to do shopping for retail therapy.

    c How do you feel about investing in the project?

    d Quentin is quite worried he would not be chosen, should he be?

10 **a** Religion is so too much full of divisions these days.

    b Zak and Zara are siblings and they live in Austria with their parents.

    c David and Jennifer had a fantastic time on their honeymoon.

    d Stella decided to shed her sophisticated image and went to the party looking like a beggar.

11 **a** Rupa and Jay come from Sri Lanka.

    b Florence is an exceptionally caring person.

    c Why on earth would you like to be a boxer?

    d She so ain't a fan of classical music.

12 **a** Concorde is such a expedient, fast plane to travel on because of its speed.

    b Taiye is one of the most sincere and serving people I know.

    c Rachel and Kenneth went on a day trip to Glasgow.

    d Judy is studying for a diploma in engineering.

13 **a** Boris has flown all over the world.

    b Tell him no to make a silly fool of himself.

    c Mrs Jabal said that Rotimi is a talented and well behaved child.

    d We have no reason to doubt the sincerity of the voluntary fundraisers.

14 **a** Cheri is a Solicitor by profession.

    b She would be certain to come on stage anytime now.

    c Bunmi and Efutubo are very close childhood friends.

    d I wonder how many countries Sonia has lived in.

15 **a** The couple are honeymooning at a secret location.

    b I respect Sam because she has a positive attitude to life.

    c There is no elevated mountain too high for Monique to climb.

    d Diana is wearing a pink, white and sky blue pullover.

16　**a**　What does a horticulturist do?

　　　b　Sally is the lady standing in the middle of the room next to Ian.

　　　c　Wayne went to Kenya on a safari holiday.

　　　d　It is simply pretentious to pretend you are the business.

17　**a**　I am pleased to meet you, Miss Campbell.

　　　b　The couple are a high profile couple.

　　　c　I have a red and black patterned housecoat.

　　　d　She has known her husband for fifteen years.

18　**a**　Jayesh is a renowned politician in his native country.

　　　b　Hilary's grandfather is the one who taught her to play the Piano.

　　　c　A'int no one tell me what to do.

　　　d　Nutritionists claim that food from fast food shops is not very nutritious.

19　**a**　I studied Typing at college so I know how to use the Keyboard for wordprocessing.

　　　b　Sheila and Verna were students together at university.

　　　c　While Cecilia was driving through Milan, she realised that a van was following her.

　　　d　My advice for you to do is to mind your own business.

20 **a** Matthew told his son Oliver that a dishwasher is used to wash utensils.

  b The bald-headed eagle is an enormously big bird.

  c The networking evening is on Monday.

  d Sally has started to learn Italian.

21 **a** Liam has decided to emigrate to China for personal reasons.

  b Christine lives and works in Munich but she is from Cologne.

  c A lot of people now go to New Guinea on holiday.

  d The grizzly bear animal is a protected few creature.

22 **a** Mano is now a student doctor. He used to work as a junior administrator.

  b A game reserve is where animal conservationists protects extremely wild animals.

  c Mr Selverajah is a very popular musician.

  d Koko is a housewife but she tells people that she is a domestic technician.

23 **a** Olyden, the photographer earn good money doing many weddings.

  b Wende is from Tanzania but she lives with her family in Paris.

  c Myriam is a medical doctor who also knows a lot about homeopathy.

  d Is Chimpanzee another name for monkey?

24 a Esther said that she would give her father flowers on fathers day.

 b We've finish building our dream house in Florida.

 c The taxidermist said that demand for his goods has diminished.

 d Benjamin played football with his friends yesterday.

TEST 3.4 *(Answers on page 198)*

Identify the best possible word to complete the sentence. Write your answer in the box. See how many you can do in 15 minutes.

1 Sean had his umbrella when she came out but he ...... got it now.

a	hasn't	**c**	shall
b	had	**d**	will

2 She was found ...... at the foot of the mountain.

a	below	**c**	unconscious
b	under	**d**	sad

3 I ...... your significant assistance.

a	envy	**c**	hope
b	ore	**d**	appreciate

4 Jordan was ...... that his son go to the best school.

   a determined   **c** lock

   b deter   **d** grow

5 Banke ...... have apologised.

   a was   **c** intend

   b going   **d** needn't

6 Jane and John ...... married next week but they have called it off.

   a were to have been   **c** going to have been

   b was   **d** were to

7 You ...... have written me a letter. I was disappointed you didn't.

   a may   **c** can

   b might   **d** would

8 I ...... you asked Cindy yourself. She does not listen to me.

   a will   **c** want that

   b want   **d** would rather

9 The road is icy and Abel was terrified lest he ...... slip.

   a will   **c** may be

   b should   **d** would had

10 Well I think that some people ...... try to cross that dangerous road.

    a will   **c** want

    b is been   **d** has

11 Christopher ...... be leaving Hong Kong tomorrow at 7 a.m.

    a shall   **c** intend

    b want   **d** hoping

12 The bed cover was made entirely by hand. It ...... taken a long time.

    a could   **c** has to

    b might   **d** must have

13 He came back from holiday with spots all over, he ...... bitten several times by mosquitoes.

    a was to have   **c** will have to have

    b must have been   **d** have been

14 ...... Tracey be here when we come back?

    a will   **c** when

    b where   **d** will be

15 People ...... waiting for that bus for a long time. It simply didn't stop.

    a may have been   **c** will be

    b must be   **d** would

16 If we hadn't had this accident we ...... home by now.

   a may go   **c** should have been

   b could go   **d** will have been going ☐

17 I got lost in Venice and ...... ask a shopkeeper the way.

   a has to   **c** had to

   b was to   **d** is to ☐

18 You ...... come here tomorrow.

   a need   **c** maybe

   b needn't   **d** went to ☐

19 We ...... pay anything for the furniture.

   a didn't have to   **c** done

   b don't   **d** no cause to ☐

20 You ...... read this novel. It is really excellent.

   a must   **c** may be

   b should know to now   **d** going to ☐

21 The young boys from the village ...... fly their kites.

   a going to   **c** are going to

   b are be going to   **d** must go to be ☐

22 ...... doing something interesting this evening?

   a shall you be going to   **c** will you be going to be

   b must you to be   **d** will you be ☐

23 When ...... putting up the price of petrol?

    a will they going to   **c** would they go to

    b will they be   **d** should they go to

24 I ...... play the piano when I was 6 years old.

    a was taught to   **c** were to be taught

    b was to taught to   **d** going to have been taught to

25 Julianna, ... the other girls in her class dislike folk music.

    a also   **c** one

    b as well as   **d** join

26 We were all ...... by the antics of the comedian.

    a amused   **c** laugh

    b joke   **d** happy

27 None of this material is ...... now, but it may be later.

    a pertinent   **c** wicked

    b now   **d** all that

28 David felt ...... because no one laughed at his joke.

    a serious   **c** astute

    b embarrassed   **d** clever

29 They ...... married women called Lucy.

    a had both   **c** would

    b want   **d** shall

30 He travelled abroad after ...... signed the contract.

  a do   **c** he is to

  b he has   **d** he had

TEST 3.5 *(Answers on page 198)*

Which of the following sentences is grammatically incorrect? Write the letter corresponding to the correct answer in the box provided. See how many you can do in 15 minutes.

1 **a** The solicitor said his client would like to make an appeal.

  b It's impossible for you to make an informed decision based on the incomplete data.

  c The man be dressed blue head to toe.

  d The techniques are designed to make you less dependent on your teacher.

2 **a** Thank you for being so supportive of me.

  b We are talking about the unjust system.

  c They need to take the responsibility away from Mr Jones.

  d You shouldn't memories bad of childhood.

3 **a** The shop has reduced the price of all its goods.

  b The company is the UK market leader.

  c The museum a'int all that.

  d We need to review our sales management process.

4 **a** The girl is twice my wait.

    b We need to send a message out to the customers.

    c Christopher Columbus discovered the Bahamas.

    d Jenny and David went to Egypt last year.

5 **a** Umberto Eco wrote the novel entitled 'The Name of The Rose'.

    b May she lend your car?

    c We have the latest gadgets at home.

    d Watch out for that careless driver.

6 **a** Bananas are also grown in Brazil.

    b Janet is liking flowers, doesn't she?

    c Will you be my date?

    d The box is very heavy to carry.

7 **a** I like going to the local post office.

    b Call me if you would like more information on direct payment.

    c He has apologised for being so silly at the party.

    d I stayed in Dubai four two weeks.

8 **a** I have decided to go to Spain with Miguel.

    b I must finish this task bye tonite.

    c I need help with my assignment.

    d She is quite clever and she knows it.

9 **a** I am very proud of you.

    b Richard is a considerate boss.

    c Try remember what has been happen.

    d My mother would like to come to England.

10 **a** I going to but didn't have the means.

    b Diamonds are mined in a few African countries.

    c Tell me the most interesting thing about you.

    d How much debt do you have?

11 **a** I have not received your letter.

    b That dress really does suit you.

    c What you put on for the wedding?

    d We have a new addition to the family.

12 **a** I am finding it difficult to concentrate in class.

    b She has a large, pink silk jacket.

    c The pyramids were built by the ancient Egyptians.

    d How you going to renovate the apartment.

13 **a** Who painted the Mona Lisa?

    b Paul went played squash with Dayo.

    c Marcia has an operation scheduled for the end of the month.

    d It is encouraging to have an understanding business partner.

14 **a** Our plan is to put an end to the strike as soon as we possibly can.

    b Benjamin went to Maldives for vacation.

    c You are not doing anything now, are you?

    d I'm paying for lunch.

15 **a** There is no point complaining because things are getting better.

    b There is not mountain two high for her to climb.

    c Turn off the lights before you leave the building.

    d How sure are you of the answers to the questions?

16 **a** I would say that to a formal acquaintance rather than a good friend.

    b Your going to be late.

    c Please leave your belongings in the hall.

    d You can only park here if you have a ticket.

17 **a** He has handed in his letter of resignation.

    b Age not my barrier for career.

    c Mr Clarke admitted to having two jobs.

    d The Lions are a much better team.

18 **a** The lion live in forests in Africa.

    b We are staying in the flat of a friend who is away for a few days.

    c I am going to the supermarket to buy some groceries.

    d A few days ago, I saw a man walking down the street.

19   **a**   I am terribly sorry I'm late.

     b   The garage is closed on Sundays.

     c   You can look up the number in the phonebook.

     d   I suppose, street crime, it same everywhere.   ☐

20   **a**   You can take some good photos with your digital camera.

     b   The zoologist study animal behaviour.

     c   I saw Mr Khan checking the stock.

     d   Linda, you must always tell the truth.   ☐

21   **a**   What material your shoe made up of.

     b   The diplomat lives in Vienna.

     c   They struck an agreement whose bitter ramifications are still being felt today.

     d   In these ideal conditions, we are having the time of our lives.   ☐

22   **a**   Sadie is fond of talking about sticking to her principles.

     b   I've bought a one little small shirt.

     c   He said that his children are obsessed with Halloween.

     d   I moved into a really small flat, a few months ago.   ☐

23   **a**   I lived with my parents for 25 years.

     b   She took the teddy bear of off me.

     c   What do you think Peter's response should be?

     d   I need to go out for a picnic with the children today.   ☐

24   **a**   He is a very sincere person.

     b   I think you are being very unreasonable.

     c   I were plaiting her hair yesterday up on to 11 p.m.

     d   I am unable to assist you because I have a lot to do today.

25   **a**   I am sorry have to have kept you waiting.

     b   I have got to get home on the bus but I have misplaced my wallet.

     c   Will you be acting in that play?

     d   He said he would leave as soon as he found another place.

26   **a**   Do you have an umbrella I can borrow?

     b   The banks are closed and I am out of money.

     c   Where do you keep your telephone?

     d   She was very extremely tired, so she stopped to take a rest.

27   **a**   Luke has never had to work because he comes from a rich family.

     b   Friendship is far more important to Richard than love.

     c   Keiran is a distinguished business man.

     d   She lost her expensively dear gold watch.

28 **a** It seems that his main problem is getting a job.

    b I am sick and tired of your arrogant attitude.

    c The antique table been in family for four generations.

    d I do hope that you can reach an amicable solution. ☐

29 **a** Mr Rajah owns the popular restaurant in the west end.

    b He drive a big large grey Jeep.

    c Ms Frost's new car runs on diesel.

    d Ms Campbell is an energetic eighty two year old. ☐

30 **a** It is important for you to increase your market share in this niche market.

    b Shoe polish used for cleaning leather shoes and many more things.

    c James had no respect for his brother.

    d He has agreed to send a large number of computers to the firm. ☐

4 VERBAL DEDUCTION

A verbal deduction test is more commonly known as a generic connection and odd-one-out test. A generic connection test is used to assess the candidate's ability to reason and identify links between words. It usually takes the form of looking for the odd one out of a given set of words. The link among/between words simply needs to be demonstrated and explanations are not usually necessary. The criteria used can be quite varied, from the general to the specific. Here are some examples: distance, age, length, weight, price, type of place, type of transportation, types of emotions, frequency, breed of animal, etc. Illustrated below is a sample test with answers and justifications.

Which word does not belong with the others?

Words

	A	B	C	D
1	floor	carpet	linoleum	curtain
2	water	filter	drink	wood
3	breath	air	pollution	grass

	A	B	C	D	E
4	love	hatred	fear	greed	anger
5	Paris	Chester	Belfast	Cardiff	Leeds

Answers			**Justification**
1	D	curtain	least associated with the others
2	D	wood	least associated with the others
3	D	grass	least associated with the others
4	A	love	love – positive emotion
	D	greed	greed – this is not an emotion
5	A	Paris	not a city in the United Kingdom

SAMPLE QUESTION: ODD-ONE-OUT

Find the odd word out among the five words. Write the letter corresponding to the correct answer in the box.

A	B	C	D	E	Answer
kitchen	oven	toilet	balcony	bedroom	**B**

The answer is oven because it is not a room in the house. So write **B** in the box.

SAMPLE QUESTION: WORD ORDER

Put the words in alphabetical order and write the answer in the boxes.

A	B	C	D	E
equipment	window	coincide	jungle	traffic

Answer | C | A | D | E | B |

In some cases you may be required to put the letters in a word in alphabetical order. The structure of the question will usually look similar to the one illustrated above. You may also be required to arrange words in alphabetical order and then identify the position of a word. Examples of such questions are illustrated below.

SAMPLE QUESTION: ALPHABETICAL ORDER

Put the letters in MISCELLANEOUS in alphabetical order.

Answer: ACEEILLMNOSSU

SAMPLE QUESTION: ALPHABETICAL POSITIONS OF WORDS

If the words in the following questions were arranged in alphabetical order, then which one would be:

		A	B	C	D	E	Answer
1	Second?	name	long	lair	fish	claw	D
2	Fourth?	coin	cold	born	less	deal	E
3	First?	alas	over	nose	ride	book	A
4	Third?	shoe	hand	foot	belt	tile	B

SAMPLE QUESTION: WORD PAIRS

There are three pairs of words. The second word of each pair has been made from the first word using the same rule for each pair. Find the rule and work out the last word for the third pair. Write your answer in the bracket.

1 port, spot; hole, shoe; kiln, (   )

The answer is 'skin'.

In the first two pairs of words, the letter 's' was added to the second word of each pair as a first letter. Then the third letter of the first word of each pair was deleted.

2 point, pint; plant, pant; prays, (   )

The answer is 'pays'.

In the first two pairs of words, the second letter of the first word in each pair was dropped in order to make the second word and the same rule must apply to the third pair.

SAMPLE QUESTION: MISSING LINK

1   What 3 letters can go before each of these to make a word?

active   create   found

The answer is 'pro'.

2   What 4 letters can go before each of these to make a word?

glide   mount   graph

The answer is 'para'.

SAMPLE QUESTION: MUDDLED LETTERS

Rearrange the muddled letters in capitals to make a proper word. The meaning of the word is given in the clue.

AGRSS   it makes a lawn

The answer is GRASS.

SAMPLE QUESTION: MISSING LETTERS AND NUMBERS

A B C D E F G H I J K L M N O P Q R S T U V W X Y Z

The alphabet has been provided to help you. Fill in the missing letters and numbers.

A1   B3   C6   D10   _____

The answer is E15 because the rule is to add an additional digit at each stage. $+2 = B$, $B + 3 = C$, $C + 4 = 10$, therefore $E = 10 + 5$.

SAMPLE QUESTION: LETTERS REPRESENTING NUMBERS

In the question below, letters represent numbers. Work out the answers to the sum and write its letter in the space provided.

If $A = 4$, $B = 6$, $C = 11$, $D = 16$, $E = 94$, what is the answer to the sum written as a letter?

$B + A \times C - E$

The answer is D.

SAMPLE QUESTION: CROSSWORDS

Fill in the crosswords so that all the words written below each grid are used. You have been provided with a letter from one of the words to give you a clue in each crossword. Here is an example:

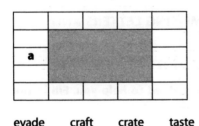

evade   craft   crate   taste

This is the solution:

c	r	a	f	t
r				a
a				s
t				t
e	v	a	d	e

TEST 4.1 *(Answers on pages 199–201)*

Put the words in alphabetical order and write your answer in the boxes. See how many you can do in 10 minutes.

	A	B	C	D	E
1	name	long	lair	fish	claw

Answer ☐☐☐☐☐

2	demilitarise	parody	entwine	eviction	trouser

Answer ☐☐☐☐☐

3	read	pass	five	cost	work

Answer ☐☐☐☐☐

4	impeccable	turbulent	parsimonious	contradictions	excursion

Answer ☐☐☐☐☐

	A	B	C	D	E
5	cash	smug	rose	trip	this

Answer

6	inarticulate	mundane	sympathise	virus	golf

Answer

7	alas	over	nose	ride	book

Answer

8	diminutive	notoriety	concoction	aplomb	stapler

Answer

9	coin	cold	born	less	deal

Answer

10	virility	enterprise	glint	shelf	orchid

Answer

11	shoe	hand	foot	belt	tile

Answer

12	cascade	militant	coincide	miserable	congestion

Answer

13	mixed	polish	angle	reporter	pollute

Answer

	A	B	C	D	E
14	chip	dark	musical	interpret	remove

Answer ☐☐☐☐

15	middle	rank	instinct	respect	director

Answer ☐☐☐☐

16	media	speculate	exchange	prevent	guide

Answer ☐☐☐☐

17	health	sauna	path	mango	exact

Answer ☐☐☐☐

18	allow	depth	evolution	deign	truant

Answer ☐☐☐☐

19	crisis	croquet	cosy	cripple	cordial

Answer ☐☐☐☐

20	usage	croak	bunch	four	fraction

Answer ☐☐☐☐

21	frame	hindmost	equator	limestone	opaque

Answer ☐☐☐☐

22	clock	enhance	committee	remunerate	public

Answer ☐☐☐☐

	A	B	C	D	E
23	legal	gabion	gait	quango	lever

Answer [ ][ ][ ]

24	heart	gypsy	hindrance	hierarchy	harmony

Answer [ ][ ][ ][ ][ ]

TEST 4.2 *(Answers on pages 201–203)*

Which word does not belong with the other three? Write the letter corresponding to the correct answer in the box. See how many you can do in 15 minutes.

	A	B	C	D	
1	floor	carpet	linoleum	curtain	[ ]
2	water	juice	drink	wood	[ ]
3	vitamin	carbohydrate	coffee	iron	[ ]
4	rain	snow	sun	hot	[ ]
5	shoe	limb	leg	road	[ ]
6	cake	curry	bread	biscuit	[ ]
7	breath	smell	inhale	cough	[ ]
8	dictate	post box	stamp	postcard	[ ]
9	duvet	bedsheet	pillow	vallance	[ ]
10	floppy disc	screen	keyboard	mouse	[ ]
11	period	minutes	hour	second	[ ]
12	pear	spinach	apple	orange	[ ]

	A	B	C	D	
13	nose	eye	fibula	mouth	☐
14	ring	bracelet	necklace	finger	☐
15	garage	toilet	spray	door	☐
16	birthday	anniversary	wedding	restaurant	☐
17	cable	speaker	receiver	volume	☐
18	dishwasher	toaster	oven	freezer	☐
19	fan	air conditioner	cooler	iron	☐
20	father	mother	daughter	boy	☐
21	nail	tongue	teeth	gum	☐
22	pupil	cornea	iris	jaw	☐
23	Paris	Abuja	Tokyo	Chester	☐
24	lecturer	writer	teacher	toastmaster	☐
25	Hindu	Islam	Christian	Disciple	☐
26	dictionary	words	explanation	translation	☐
27	rain	pour	damp	spring	☐
28	shirt	blouse	bracelet	trouser	☐
29	rugby	football	badminton	polo	☐
30	up	wider	elevate	higher	☐
31	zip	cotton	wool	polyester	☐
32	bass	artist	soprano	tenor	☐
33	work	holiday	vacation	break	☐
34	heart	core	centre	judge	☐
35	advance	applaud	progress	improve	☐

	A	B	C	D	
36	chalk	blackboard	duster	surgery	☐
37	waiter	cooker	driver	menu	☐
38	cotton	acrylic	silk	wool	☐
39	thyme	mint	parsley	garlic	☐
40	razor	knife	scissors	spoon	☐

TEST 4.3 *(Answers on page 203)*

What 2 letters can go before each of these to make a word? Write your answer in the box. See how many you can do in 5 minutes.

1	tangle	list	joy	☐
2	together	ways	though	☐
3	camp	case	circle	☐
4	compose	commission	code	☐
5	count	cover	course	☐
6	vice	way	where	☐
7	bow	tail	blood	☐
8	call	cap	assure	☐
9	form	face	fault	☐
10	close	courage	chain	☐
11	tension	temperate	supportable	☐
12	value	sign	unite	☐
13	change	mouth	moor	☐

14	voice	visible	vulnerable	
15	head	half	gun	

TEST 4.4 *(Answers on page 204)*

What 3 letters can go before each of these to make a word? Write your answer in the box. See how many you can do in 10 minutes.

1	force	filter	hostess	
2	secret	spin	up	
3	appear	allow	agree	
4	stop	stick	starter	
5	break	book	care	
6	line	head	path	
7	giver	less	breaker	
8	handle	grove	hole	
9	net	land	pike	
10	place	lay	print	
11	hive	keeper	line	
12	mask	ring	plant	
13	smoker	sense	resident	
14	appoint	approve	arm	
15	sail	soil	side	
16	snip	take	son	

17	colour	charge	content	
18	horse	mill	dust	
19	locate	loyal	miss	
20	bug	room	bath	

TEST 4.5 *(Answers on page 204)*

What 4 letters can go before each of these to make a word? Write your answer in the box. See how many you can do in 10 minutes.

1	going	chair	money	
2	space	drome	plane	
3	paper	pit	bag	
4	shop	plan	house	
5	sitter	carriage	wipe	
6	septic	racism	perspirant	
7	hold	man	way	
8	storm	water	trap	
9	ship	start	on	
10	ground	bench	bone	
11	lace	line	wear	
12	flow	head	due	
13	rooted	sea	freeze	
14	guard	keeping	house	

15	back	faced	foot	
16	power	seas	ride	
17	out	up	with	
18	site	psychology	meter	
19	crier	ship	hall	
20	seat	period	conduct	

TEST 4.6 *(Answers on page 204)*

What 5 letters can go before each of these to make a word? Write your answer in the box. See how many you can do in 5 minutes.

1	tennis	mountain	licence	
2	alley	spot	trust	
3	agent	release	box	
4	out	release	vote	
5	down	even	in	
6	less	mate	room	
7	guard	berry	mail	
8	storey	stage	processor	
9	cloth	spoon	ware	
10	gage	grocer	house	
11	brush	paste	ache	
12	group	donor	brother	

TEST 4.7 *(Answers on pages 204–205)*

Which letter can be moved from the first word to the second word to make two new words? The letters must not otherwise be rearranged and both new words must make sense. See how many you can do in 8 minutes.

1	cup	love	_____ _____ _____
2	hall	at	_____ _____ _____
3	gape	one	_____ _____ _____
4	charm	oil	_____ _____ _____
5	when	arm	_____ _____ _____
6	kit	in	_____ _____ _____
7	pride	ore	_____ _____ _____
8	tart	able	_____ _____ _____
9	place	ace	_____ _____ _____
10	peel	at	_____ _____ _____
11	pear	ink	_____ _____ _____
12	box	ore	_____ _____ _____
13	tape	all	_____ _____ _____
14	shoe	lap	_____ _____ _____

15 bend   and   _____ _____ _____

16 frank   low   _____ _____ _____

17 pinch   ore   _____ _____ _____

18 glass   lobe   _____ _____ _____

19 probe   act   _____ _____ _____

20 cape   up   _____ _____ _____

TEST 4.8 *(Answers on page 205)*

Time allowed: 10 minutes

If the words in the following questions were arranged in alphabetical order, then which one would be:

	A	**B**	**C**	**D**	**E**	Answer
1 First?	make	scent	said	wake	move	☐
2 Third?	first	sign	once	point	plane	☐
3 Second?	below	begin	last	save	take	☐
4 First?	silver	walk	slide	quick	monk	☐
5 Fifth?	wind	person	worth	wait	weigh	☐
6 Third?	early	bush	idea	large	bird	☐
7 Fourth?	best	alter	foster	model	quench	☐

		A	**B**	**C**	**D**	**E**	Answer
8	Fourth?	tired	doll	wise	pupil	lorry	☐
9	Second?	task	female	free	plan	voice	☐
10	First?	world	able	taxi	kite	access	☐
11	Fifth?	brush	bake	speak	set	view	☐
12	Third?	elect	lend	permit	prompt	prose	☐
13	Third?	clock	charge	case	cause	cast	☐
14	Second?	pretty	basic	blue	belt	apart	☐
15	Fifth?	spot	shore	stone	strike	spoke	☐
16	Fifth?	angel	phone	fake	fur	please	☐
17	Second?	trip	type	topic	tame	take	☐
18	Second	smug	rose	cash	soap	april	☐
19	Third?	tile	pay	clock	aim	phone	☐
20	Fourth?	feet	fake	fur	fore	pick	☐
21	Second?	over	hay	hand	shoe	pack	☐
22	Third?	nose	navel	work	ride	mate	☐
23	Fifth?	allow	alas	belt	book	ace	☐
24	Third?	cold	case	work	less	deal	☐

TEST 4.9 *(Answers on pages 205–207)*

Put the letters in the following words in alphabetical order. Write the answer on the line. See how many you can do in 15 minutes.

1 stairwell _____

2 marginalise _____

3 resistance _____

4 guerrilla _____

5 neurology _____

6 cautious _____

7 terrorism _____

8 satellite _____

9 cantankerous _____

10 flamboyant _____

11 exception _____

12 illustration _____

13 telescope _____

14 assertive _____

15 exemplary _____

16 invaded _____

17 independent _____

18 mastery _____

19 washington _____

20 fundamental _____

21 scientific _____

22 paragliding _____

23 consequence _____

24 paralytic _____

25 encouragement _____

26 durability _____

27 access _____

28 fusion _____

29 locum _____

30 logistics _____

31 television	_____	**36** category	_____
32 advance	_____	**37** alternately	_____
33 envelope	_____	**38** independent	_____
34 probability	_____	**39** coastline	_____
35 downcast	_____	**40** dragonfly	_____

TEST 4.10 *(Answers on pages 207–208)*

Rearrange the muddled letters in capitals to make a proper word. The meaning of the word is given in the clue.
Write the word in the space provided. See how many you can do in 10 minutes.

1 EUORSGNE   Willing to give or share.   _____

2 OLLRTEY   This is used to put things in when in supermarkets.   _____

3 NKAPCAE   Thin cake made from batter.   _____

4 ETNALRN   This can be used instead of a candle.   _____

5 TASCEL   The aristocrats live in such places.   _____

6 TLOMIPIE   This is not being cordial.   _____

7 UCIFIDFLT   This is not easy.   _____

8 RABYEKOD   A piano and a computer has one of these.   _____

9 LDEOSM   This is another word for occasionally.   _____

10 INSXPEEVE   This means something is very dear.   _____

11 IRTAANTCC   The area around the South Pole.   _____

12 AREOCUG   We need it to face our fears.   _____

13 RUBTACST   This means to make a reduction.   _____

14 EPNEOLVE   Something used to wrap or cover a letter before posting.   _____

15 TRSAPAIE   Organism that lives and feeds on others.   _____

16 RATBSOCDA   To transmit on radio or television.   _____

17 RIBHADTY   The day someone was born.   _____

18 PLOALG   The fastest gait of a horse.   _____

19 RTPNMAATE   A flat in a building.   _____

20 NGLTELNIETI   Being clever.   _____

TEST 4.11 _(Answers on page 208)_

In the questions below, letters represent numbers. Work out the answers to the sum and write its letter in the space provided. See how many you can do in 10 minutes.

1 If A = 2, B = 4, C = 10, D = 8, E = 1. $C \times D \div B \div A =$ ☐

2 If A = 24, B = 69, C = 27, D = 28, E = 4. $(B + C) \div E =$ ☐

3 If A = 22, B = 14, C = 6, D = 8, E = 1. $(A + B \times E) \div C =$ ☐

4 If A = 5, B = 4, C = 10, D = 25, E = 20. $(D \times B) \div E =$ ☐

5 If A = 39, B = 31, C = 35, D = 3, E = 1. $(B + A) \div C + E =$ ☐

6 If A = 87, B = 20, C = 4, D = 8, E = 13. $(A + E) \times C \div B =$ ☐

7 If A = 16, B = 36, C = 27, D = 4, E = 2. $(B + A + E) \div E =$ ☐

8 If A = 62, B = 35, C = 65, D = 44, E = 6. $(A + D) - E - C =$ ☐

9 If A = 2, B = 7, C = 10, D = 6, E = 4. $((A \times B) + C) \div E =$ ☐

10 If A = 88, B = 4, C = 2, D = 3, E = 5. $((A \div B) - C) \div E =$ ☐

11 If A = 2, B = 34, C = 17, D = 23, E = 12. $B + E \div A =$ ☐

12 If A = 7, B = 65, C = 47, D = 8, E = 11. $C + E + A =$ ☐

13 If A = 62, B = 75, C = 32, D = 19, E = 31. $(C + A) - D =$ ☐

14 If A = 39, B = 31, C = 29, D = 9, E = 11. $(C + A + B) \div E =$ ☐

15 If A = 21, B = 45, C = 24, D = 10, E = 17. $B + A + C - B =$ ☐

16 If A = 5, B = 15, C = 30, D = 18, E = 20. $B - A + E =$ ☐

17 If A = 72, B = 24, C = 42, D = 45, E = 2. $(A - B + C) \div E =$ ☐

18 If A = 92, B = 74, C = 22, D = 48, E = 8. $D + B - E - C =$ ☐

19 If A = 66, B = 78, C = 10, D = 14, E = 4. $(B - E + A) \div D =$ ☐

20 If A = 21, B = 19, C = 20, D = 5, E = 12. $C + A + B \div E =$ ☐

TEST 4.12 *(Answers on page 208)*

In the questions below, you must move one letter from the word on the left to the word on the right to make two new words. You must not rearrange the letters. See how many you can do in 10 minutes.

1 ore	on	_____	_____
2 horse	tea	_____	_____
3 warm	it	_____	_____
4 plant	pace	_____	_____
5 grime	chap	_____	_____
6 brush	tip	_____	_____
7 son	hotel	_____	_____
8 shop	eat	_____	_____
9 hope	ant	_____	_____
10 feel	heath	_____	_____
11 hat	ash	_____	_____
12 blank	ace	_____	_____
13 stall	ink	_____	_____
14 note	tar	_____	_____
15 plan	ice	_____	_____
16 off	old	_____	_____
17 hear	at	_____	_____

18 tall	act	_____	_____
19 pan	ink	_____	_____
20 flip	lame	_____	_____

TEST 4.13 *(Answers on page 209)*

A B C D E F G H I J K L M N O P Q R S T U V W X Y Z

The alphabet above has been written out to help you to fill in the missing letters and numbers. See how many you can do in 10 minutes.

1 Az	By	Cx	Dw	_____
2 B2	D4	F6	_____	J10
3 Za	_____	Xc	Wd	Ve
4 A	D	_____	J	M
5 _____	Gb	Hc	Id	Je
6 O1	Q3	S5	_____	W9
7 C10	_____	F25	G30	J45
8 A13	C39	_____	F78	G91
9 K21	L28	M35	N42	_____
10 _____	Ui	Vj	Wk	Xl
11 A6	_____	C14	D18	E22
12 L15	M31	N48	_____	P85
13 Ea	Gc	_____	Kg	Mi

14 Oa	Nb	Mc	Ld	_____
15 S15	T31	U48	V66	_____
16 Lq	Mr	_____	Ot	Pu
17 Z60	X48	V36	T24	_____
18 A3	C6	E9	G12	_____
19 F70	G61	H52	_____	J36
20 C1	_____	I3	L4	O5

TEST 4.14 *(Answers on pages 209–211)*

Fill in the crosswords so that all the words written below each grid are used. You have been provided with a letter from one of the words to give you a clue in each crossword. See how many you can do in 20 minutes.

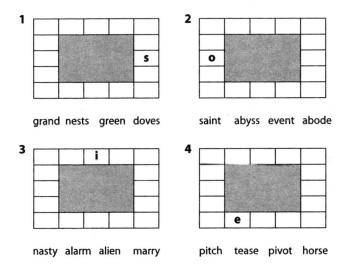

1

grand nests green doves

2

saint abyss event abode

3

nasty alarm alien marry

4

pitch tease pivot horse

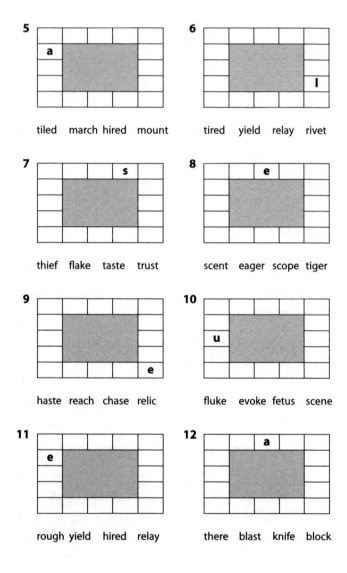

5

tiled   march   hired   mount

6

tired   yield   relay   rivet

7

thief   flake   taste   trust

8

scent   eager   scope   tiger

9

haste   reach   chase   relic

10

fluke   evoke   fetus   scene

11

rough   yield   hired   relay

12

there   blast   knife   block

13

a				

risky   maize   entry   miner

14

				o

pinch   evade   place   house

15

	r			

class   score   cross   skate

16

			n	

apply   diary   salad   sauna

17

			i	

point   beach   thigh   plumb

18

	w			

duvet   tacit   faint   dwarf

19

n				

drift   knife   drink   trade

20

		a		

rhyme   stair   movie   steam

TEST 4.15 *(Answers on pages 211–213)*

Put the letters in the following words in alphabetical order. Write the answer on the line. See how many you can do in 15 minutes.

1	mineralizer	_____	**21** quadrilateral	_____
2	chromosone	_____	**22** pulverisation	_____
3	exfoliate	_____	**23** rectification	_____
4	sociobiology	_____	**24** backlighted	_____
5	ecosystem	_____	**25** milliseconds	_____
6	synchroneity	_____	**26** semiconductor	_____
7	reclamation	_____	**27** degradation	_____
8	percolate	_____	**28** elongation	_____
9	orientation	_____	**29** enhancement	_____
10	sedimentary	_____	**30** wattages	_____
11	paradigms	_____	**31** shuttle	_____
12	monogenetic	_____	**32** pneumatic	_____
13	memorialize	_____	**33** accreditation	_____
14	overrunning	_____	**34** preliminary	_____
15	particulate	_____	**35** appellant	_____
16	pastoralist	_____	**36** multidisciplinary	_____
17	pioneer	_____	**37** proprietary	_____
18	recombination	_____	**38** censorship	_____
19	radioactivity	_____	**39** responsory	_____
20	reverberation	_____	**40** processional	_____

5 VERBAL ANALOGIES

Verbal analogy tests the candidate's knowledge of simple verbal relationships. An analogy is two words with a direct relationship. Concepts are linked in pairs and you need to identify the relationship. Some of these relationships are as follows:

SYNONYMS

Synonyms are words with the same or similar meaning. The questions assess your knowledge of words and you will be required to identify words with the same meaning. Below is a list of such words:

Word	Similar word	Word	Similar word
abandon	leave	current	fashionable
abroad	overseas	defend	safeguard
alone	single	deluxe	superior
bitter	acrid	durable	long lasting
buy	purchase	crisis	dilemma
collapse	fall apart	doomed	condemned

It will be necessary for you to memorise and use as many of these words as possible.

ANTONYMS

Antonyms are words with opposite meaning. The test will require you to identify such words. Examples of antonyms are included in the list of words below:

Word	Opposite	Word	Opposite
ban	permit	criticise	praise
broad-minded	prejudiced	definite	vague
dressy	casual	enter	go out
enable	inhibit	exhale	breathe in
cynical	believing	fidget	be still

There are other relationships between words, some of these are categorised thus:

- **cause and effect** – e.g. 'gluttony' is to 'overweight'
- **order/sequence** – e.g. 'autumn' is to 'winter'
- **'is a place where'** – e.g. 'church' is to 'vicar'
- **degree** – e.g. 'warm' is to 'cold'
- **'is used to'** – e.g. 'knife' is to 'cut'
- **groups** – e.g. 'blue' is to 'yellow'
- **part to whole** – e.g. 'child' is to 'family'

This list is not exhaustive and the relationship is usually quite basic. A thesaurus of synonyms and antonyms is a good source of reference. Examples of such relationships and how the link is expressed is illustrated below:

- addendum is to addenda as alumnus is to alumni;
- bid is to bade as break is to broke;
- billy goat is to nanny goat as bridegroom is to bride;
- buck is to doe as bull is to cow;
- butter is to milk as iron is to ore;
- cock is to hen as colt is to filly;
- far is to farther as good is to better;
- landlord is to landlady as widower is to widow;

- leather is to skin as wood is to paper;
- lord is to lady as hero is to heroine;
- thesis is to theses as phenomenon is to phenomena;
- word is to letter as music is to note.

Verbal analogy questions are presented in various formats and the main ones are illustrated below. The same question has been presented differently in the first two formats.

SAMPLE QUESTION: FORMAT 1

Finger is to hand as sentence is to:

a paragraph

b phrase

c book

d memorandum

Answer: The correct answer is **a** because the progression is to bigger units.

SAMPLE QUESTION: FORMAT 2

OUNCE:POUND = SENTENCE: _____

a paragraph   **b** sharp   **c** book   **d** memorandum

Answer: The correct answer is **a** because the progression is to bigger units.

SAMPLE QUESTION: FORMAT 3

Two words are presented on one line and the candidate is expected to choose two words from a lower line, one from each half.

	NIGHT			**DAY**	
Dark	Humid	Moonlight	Rain	Light	Windy

Answer: The correct options are 'dark' and 'light', as from the choice available, there is an obvious link with the relationship to the words on the first line. It is dark at night and light during the day.

SAMPLE QUESTION: FORMAT 4

Find two words, one from each group, that are closest in meaning.

raise	level	step
high	elevate	lower

A	**B**	**C**	**D**	Answer
raise	step	lower	step	[A]
elevate	lower	level	high	

There are other variations to these formats but the idea is generally the same. There now follows some practice tests.

TEST 5.1 *(Answers on page 214)*

Which of the following words is closest in meaning to the words in capitals. Write the letter in the box. See how many you can do in 15 minutes.

1 METAMORPHOSE

   a hurricane

   b transform

   c printer

   d wrist

2 CONCISE

   a short

   b chalk

   c candle

   d torch

3 UNFOUNDED

   a restore

   b baseless

   c divert

   d boil

4 INSIGNIA

   a true

   b emblem

   c doodle

   d stencil

5 COLOSSAL

   a game

   b huge

   c deflate

   d freeze

6 LIKE

   a analogous

   b capable

   c destitute

   d disallow

7 PROMPTITUDE

   a alacrity

   b when

   c welcome

   d upright ☐

8 HUSBANDRY

   a quill

   b agriculture

   c pond

   d oxen ☐

9 INTENSIFY

   a lantern

   b elbow

   c aggravate

   d miner ☐

10 SCHEDULE

   a sight

   b draft

   c agenda

   d main ☐

11 DRESS

   a gown

   b exclude

   c alert

   d show ☐

12 HAPPY-GO-LUCKY

   a cedar

   b carefree

   c hockey

   d pine ☐

13 AUDACIOUS

   a ton

   b bold

   c worker

   d infant ☐

14 COMMENCE

   a begin

   b interest

   c control

   d expect ☐

15 ALLEVIATE

   a practice

   b visual

   c relieve

   d accurate ☐

16 CONGENIAL

   a fluency

   b pleasant

   c critical

   d assess ☐

17 BELVEDERE

   a suitable

   b summerhouse

   c reason

   d business ☐

18 OVERWHELMED

   a pursuit

   b aghast

   c generate

   d administer ☐

19 ELDERLINESS

   a consume

   b caducity

   c strong

   d recognise ☐

20 REPEATEDLY

   a accurate

   b frequently

   c designed

   d quality ☐

21 ACCUMULATION

   a plate

   b amassment

   c announcement

   d naval ☐

22 DETRIMENTAL

   a ale

   b unfavourable

   c programme

   d reek ☐

23 OPULENT

   a weather

   b affluent

   c transfer

   d pride

24 EXONERATE

   a course

   b vindicate

   c pearl

   d per cent

25 COMMEND

   a check

   b applaud

   c power

   d glue

26 UNDERTAKE

   a approximate

   b please

   c promise

   d require

27 BEST

   a top

   b hard

   c account

   d whisper

28 UNPALATABLE

   a subtract

   b wallet

   c distasteful

   d watchful

29 GAMESOME

   a estimate

   b wire

   c swimming

   d playful

30 PRIVY

   a clock

   b private

   c entrance

   d ballot

31 CONFRONT

   a stakeholder

   b face

   c context

   d real

32 ASSERT

   a experience

   b affirm

   c denote

   d subordinate

33 FRIGHTEN

   a quality

   b scare

   c individual

   d expert

34 ACKNOWLEDGE

   a collect

   b concede

   c structure

   d environment

35 EXECUTE

   a perform

   b before

   c exact

   d evolve

36 ASSIMILATE

   a absorb

   b explain

   c concern

   d equate

37 ACQUIRE

   a procure

   b send

   c deliberate

   d guide

38 HOPEFUL

   a limited

   b optimistic

   c sadly

   d embark

39 PRODUCTIVE

   a propose

   b fertile

   c read

   d section

40 SHARE

   a cognitive

   b partake

   c anxiety

   d insight

TEST 5.2 *(Answers on page 215)*

Find the word that is closest in meaning to the word in capitals. Write your answer in the box. See how many you can do in 9 minutes.

1 QUICK

A	B	C	D	E
slow	catch	rapid	cross	canvass

2 COMMENCE

A	B	C	D	E
begin	work	finish	execute	type

3 REDUCE

A	B	C	D	E
plan	decrease	grow	small	topic

4 ENOUGH

A	B	C	D	E
gain	tough	wheel	sufficient	dice

5 MISTAKE

A	B	C	D	E
tick	error	correct	right	done

6 IMPORTANT

A	B	C	D	E
weigh	watch	bend	ace	vital

7 COURAGEOUS

A	B	C	D	E
brave	afford	scare	soul	might

8 COMPETE

A	B	C	D	E
gone	race	left	aim	actual

9 PIERCE

A	B	C	D	E
probe	rub	twist	puncture	sharp

10 ROBE

A	B	C	D	E
short	drill	bought	trouser	dress

11 DOMESTICATED

A	B	C	D	E
trendy	homely	vogue	tight	cookery

12 UNDERMINE

A	B	C	D	E
upgrade	intent	belittle	being	natural

13 DEFIANT

A	B	C	D	E
rely	ready	obvious	rebellious	tolerate

14 ATTACH

A	B	C	D	E
tame	initial	train	tap	affix

15 POLITE

A	B	C	D	E
cordial	happy	motivate	assist	dwell

16 BASIS

A	B	C	D	E
ground	weed	boiler	chest	found

17 GATHER

A	B	C	D	E
refrain	allow	collect	attempt	deliver

18 PASS

A	B	C	D	E
acquit	assess	succeed	domain	repay

19 ANTICIPATE

A	B	C	D	E
delay	drive	expect	format	drop

20 MEDIOCRE

A	B	C	D	E
excite	medium	tool	revolve	reinstate

21 VALUABLE

A	B	C	D	E
priceless	reason	rotate	respect	approach

22 PEACEFUL

A	B	C	D	E
tranquil	equip	temper	donate	evolve

23 HAGGLE

A	B	C	D	E
remorse	eloquent	redeem	negotiate	whisper

24 CHEAP

A	B	C	D	E
arch	inexpensive	bridge	costly	change

TEST 5.3 *(Answers on page 215)*

Which of the following words is opposite in meaning to the words in capitals. Write the letter in the box. See how many you can do in 8 minutes.

1 OCCUPIED

   a left

   b against

   c free

   d refute

2 HYPOTHETICAL

   a suggest

   b potential

   c concrete

   d expect

3 REJECT

   a refuse

   b approve

   c gentle

   d awake

4 DISAGREEABLE

   a nice

   b pleasant

   c mobile

   d enjoy

5 ALLEVIATE

   a heighten

   b radio

   c thesis

   d police

6 DETACH

   a fix

   b circle

   c marrow

   d heat

7 INACTIVE

   a holiday

   b nimble

   c report

   d could

8 WEALTHY

   a sank

   b impecunious

   c flowers

   d precise

9 APPRECIATE

   a bedding

   b devalue

   c choice

   d portion

10 TRANQUILISE

   a agitate

   b glass

   c handle

   d result

11 SKILFUL

   a incompetent

   b rather

   c horrify

   d provide ☐

12 INDULGE

   a curb

   b green

   c game

   d perform ☐

13 INTREPID

   a cowardly

   b imagination

   c convince

   d doubt ☐

14 IMPEDE

   a technical

   b help

   c defence

   d walk ☐

15 WITHHOLD

   a bid

   b ultimately

   c grant

   d problem ☐

16 TERRIFY

   a length

   b tournament

   c important

   d embolden ☐

17 COMPARABLE

   a finance

   b govern

   c personal

   d different ☐

18 CONVICT

   a exonerate

   b promote

   c excuse

   d popular ☐

19 END

   a difficult

   b paragraph

   c coverage

   d inaugurate ☐

20 MAJUSCULE

   a countries

   b minuscule

   c concern

   d points ☐

TEST 5.4 *(Answers on pages 215–216)*

Which of the following words is opposite in meaning to the words in capitals. Write the letter in the box. See how many you can do in 8 minutes.

1 IMITATION

   a bold

   b original

   c misfit

   d occupy ☐

2 EXIT

   a perturb

   b enter

   c lure

   d variant ☐

3 HORIZONTAL

   a spicy

   b curved

   c vertical

   d pointed ☐

4 ERROR

   a tick

   b know

   c correct

   d check ☐

5 RETENTION

 a remake

 b relinquishment

 c respect

 d donate ☐

6 CREDIT

 a statement

 b debit

 c cheque

 d client ☐

7 RECEIPT

 a paper

 b payment

 c card

 d booklet ☐

8 DISSATISFACTION

 a contentment

 b charge

 c boom

 d classic ☐

9 BEAUTY

 a ugliness

 b herbal

 c nutrition

 d youth ☐

10 HUMILITY

 a haughtiness

 b age

 c tongue

 d calmness ☐

11 ARRANGEMENT

 a untidiness

 b cold

 c united

 d gather ☐

12 SOBER

 a laugh

 b drunk

 c paint

 d blame ☐

13 NATURAL

   a consume

   b synthetic

   c taunt

   d playful ☐

14 SOLUTION

   a problem

   b desk

   c phone

   d dice ☐

15 BORROW

   a shake

   b lend

   c rope

   d beg ☐

16 DEAR

   a cheap

   b expensive

   c desire

   d valley ☐

17 PLEASURE

   a depart

   b claim

   c outspoken

   d pain ☐

18 REJOICE

   a brochure

   b happy

   c lament

   d chorus ☐

19 OPTIMISM

   a upbeat

   b pessimism

   c hopeful

   d enjoy ☐

20 PENALTY

   a consult

   b forfeit

   c adequate

   d reward ☐

TEST 5.5 *(Answers on page 216)*

Find the word that is opposite in meaning to the word in capitals. Write your answer in the box. See how many you can do in 9 minutes.

1 CLERGY **Answer**

A	B	C	D	E
relax	profession	priest	teach	laity

2 SELL

A	B	C	D	E
purchase	auction	vendor	broker	price

3 LEGAL

A	B	C	D	E
lawyer	unlawful	locate	fund	civil

4 DECENCY

A	B	C	D	E
nice	judge	obscenity	soil	obscure

5 FASTING

A	B	C	D	E
volume	lunch	dinner	length	gluttony

6 VIRTUE

A	B	C	D	E
vice	patience	adore	advocate	listener

7 INNOCENCE

A	B	C	D	E
pure	joyful	guilt	mirror	court

8 SACRIFICING

A	B	C	D	E
important	together	across	ungenerous	enough

9 DISAPPROVE

A	B	C	D	E
like	people	comic	programme	assume

10 PREROGATIVE

A	B	C	D	E
heritage	infancy	unprivileged	development	pacific

11 PHILANTHROPY

A	B	C	D	E
forget	monopoly	misanthropy	errand	relative

12 FONDNESS

A	B	C	D	E
calf	hatred	medicine	methodology	spread

13 RASHNESS

A	B	C	D	E
glasses	joint	unanimous	caution	slipper

14 TIMID

A	B	C	D	E
polite	void	courageous	oppose	wealthy

15 WIT

A	B	C	D	E
metropole	dullness	impress	isolate	physical

16 TRANQUIL

A	B	C	D	E
straight	cautious	available	excessive	turbulent

17 HARD

A	B	C	D	E
statement	ceremony	insular	soft	influence

18 EXPENDITURE

A	B	C	D	E
hospitable	income	honest	against	common

19 FORTUNE

A	B	C	D	E
indelible	election	poverty	central	role

20 PROFIT

A	B	C	D	E
loss	support	veto	gap	flag

21 EXCLUDE

A	B	C	D	E
reform	hospitable	character	morale	include

22 FREEDOM

A	B	C	D	E
bondage	favour	hinted	step	down

23 SEVERITY

A	B	C	D	E
proceed	perceives	study	leniency	concern

24 PROSPERITY

A	B	C	D	E
constitution	referendum	journalist	arrest	adversity

TEST 5.6 *(Answers on page 217)*

You have been provided with two words in capital letters that are related in some way. You have also been given a third word in capital letters that has a similar relationship with one of the options you have been provided with in the lower line. Your task is to identify the word and write your answer in the box provided. See how many you can do in 9 minutes.

1 STUDY:STUDENT = TEACH:

A	B	C	D	E
teacher	read	literate	pupil	clever

2 WELSH:WALES = GERMAN:

A	B	C	D	E
dutch	germany	colony	spain	dublin

3 SUN:SHINES = WIND:

A	B	C	D	E
eruption	lightning	breeze	cool	blows

4 ONE:FIRST = TEN:

A	B	C	D	E
days	tenth	position	eleven	times

5 LESS:MORE = LITTLE:

A	B	C	D	E
much	small	petite	elevate	amount

6 CARD:DECK = PLAYER:

A	B	C	D	E
people	team	label	together	utopia

7 ASK:RECEIVE = SEEK:

A	B	C	D	E
sift	thrill	demand	find	look

8 EAT:EATEN = READ:

A	B	C	D	E
encript	read	note	letter	write

9 CHINA:CHINESE = SPAIN

A	B	C	D	E
dialect	speak	spaniard	madrid	spanish

10 KILN:POTTERY = OVEN:

A	B	C	D	E
fridge	cake	dryer	milk	yeast

11 TALL:SHORT = STRONG:

A	B	C	D	E
dominate	loud	slight	weak	lanky

12 MUSICIAN:MUSIC = SCIENCE:

A	B	C	D	E
scientist	discovery	predict	learn	acquire

13 NORTH:SOUTH = RICH:

A	B	C	D	E
east	west	show	grand	poor

14 LEAF:LEAVES = FINGER:

A	B	C	D	E
dry	autumn	lady	fingers	green

15 TRUE:FALSE = EAST:

A	B	C	D	E
directive	follow	west	sweat	explore

16 ART:ARTIST = BUILD:

A	B	C	D	E
builder	construct	brick	demonstrate	sell

17 CAR:DRIVER = AEROPLANE:

A	B	C	D	E
fly	pilot	control	tower	airport

18 SHIP:CARGO = TRAIN:

A	B	C	D	E
freight	things	boxes	courier	postage

19 HERBIVORE:VEGETABLE = CARNIVORE:

A	B	C	D	E
chick	meat	mince	chops	diced

20 HOUSE:PERSON = CAGE:

A	B	C	D	E
bird	hut	robin	mouse	eagle

□

21 LION:CUB = HEN:

A	B	C	D	E
chick	cockerel	dog	cat	eggs

□

22 YOU:YOURS = I:

A	B	C	D	E
me	her	mine	him	one

□

23 1ST:FIRST = 11TH:

A	B	C	D	E
tenth	eleventh	twelfth	eleven	second

□

24 EARS:HEAR = TONGUE:

A	B	C	D	E
look	like	stew	move	taste

□

TEST 5.7 *(Answers on page 217)*

You have been provided with an incomplete statement. Your task is to identify the word from the four options provided that best completes the phrase. Write your answer in the box provided. See how many you can do in 9 minutes.

1 Newspaper is to reader as ...... is to listener.

    a decision   **c** asylum

    b foil   **d** radio

□

2 Won is to one as ...... is to wait.

   a expensive   **c** legal

   b weight   **d** gravy

3 Moisturise is to skin as ...... is to shoes.

   a lithuanian   **c** polish

   b vendor   **d** code

4 Leg is to person as ...... is to car.

   a quit   **c** exclusive

   b wheel   **d** committee

5 Kilogramme is to weight as ...... is to length.

   a recommend   **c** metre

   b transparency   **d** exclusive

6 Boy is to lad as ...... is to lass.

   a delighted   **c** girl

   b ambition   **d** posh

7 Sheep is to mutton as ...... is to pork.

   a bonus   **c** cat

   b pig   **d** enjoy

8 Student is to study as ...... is to rehearse.

   a numerous   **c** actor

   b message   **d** attempt

9 Clock is to time as ...... is to temperature.

   a theatre   **c** thermometer

   b particular   **d** detective

10 Ticket is to theatre as ...... is to country.

   a macho   **c** visa

   b grassroots   **d** huddles

11 Password is to computer as ...... is to door.

   a stomach   **c** skipper

   b key   **d** spinal

12 Victory is to defeat as ...... is to sad.

   a passengers   **c** happy

   b authorities   **d** rescue

13 Snapper is to scale as ...... is to feather.

   a groan   **c** squid

   b owl   **d** assembly

14 Cock is to hen as ...... is to female.

   a collaborator   **c** static

   b male   **d** prestigious

15 England is to pound as ...... is to rand.

   a conservative   **c** south africa

   b accra   **d** provence

16 Sun is to rain as ...... is to wet.

   a candid   **c** exact

   b dry   **d** propel

17 Ring is to finger as ...... is to wrist.

   a intellect   **c** bracelet

   b quality   **d** lousy

18 Book is to read as ...... is to watch.

   a associate   **c** mirror

   b pebble   **d** television

19 Cot is to bed as ...... is to adult.

   a erstwhile   **c** linen

   b baby   **d** vertigo

20 Income is to expenditure as ...... is to liability.

   a squirrel   **c** chores

   b asset   **d** inspire

21 Painter is to canvas as sculptor is to ......

   a official   **c** vintage

   b marble   **d** spectator

22 Door is to room as ...... is to hold.

    a initiate   **c** intimate

    b hatch   **d** windfall

23 Child is to adult as ...... is to pig.

    a taint   **c** piglet

    b colossal   **d** explore

24 Detergent is to clothes as ...... is to skin.

    a arena   **c** guard

    b soap   **d** dexterity

TEST 5.8 *(Answers on pages 218–221)*

You have been provided with two words in capital letters that are related in some way. You have also been given six words on the lower line, three in each half. Your task is to identify two words, one from each half that forms a verbal analogy when paired with the words in the upper line. Record your answer by underlining the two words. See how many you can do in 15 minutes.

1	BED			SLEEP	
cup	trunk	chair	duvet	drink	pillow

2	EMPLOYED			UNEMPLOYED	
field	plant	sow	wheat	grass	fallow

3	SLICE			BREAD	
part	bake	divide	cake	number	mouse

4	BONE			HORSE	
joint	fish	steak	wolf	meat	fishbones

5	FRANCE			ENGLAND	
Lille	Paris	Lyon	London	Durban	Dublin

6	INCOME			EXPENDITURE	
spend	debit	expense	credit	borrow	grant

7	CIPHER			CRACK	
mystery	click	check	amuse	dawn	unriddle

8	WEEK			DAYS	
time	wallet	minute	image	seconds	tense

9	PLANE			AIR	
jump	ship	search	sea	security	amend

10	ACTOR			STAGE	
tennis player	engage	donate	watch	shout	court

11	SPINACH			TOMATO	
pepper	soup	green	red	cabbage	blue

12	COLLEGE			UNIVERSITY	
taught	teacher	uniform	place	nanny	lecturer

13	START			FINISH	
beginning	approach	swell	ache	cause	end

14	KNIFE			PENCIL	
scoop	cutting	chop	train	mould	writing

15	FOOTBALLER			PITCH	
kite	bought	dancer	transfer	floor	manage

16	TONGUE			TASTE	
nose	move	speak	hear	allow	smell

17	TRAIN			TRACK	
transport	pedestrian	voyage	footpath	leisure	stroll

18	EYES			VISION	
legs	glasses	magnify	acrobat	suspend	motion

19	APPLE			CABBAGE	
ferry	fruit	save	some	component	vegetable

20	LAWN TENNIS			RACKET	
ace	table tennis	fruit	bat	score	operator

21	MONARCH			SUBJECT	
seat	master	throne	genuine	experience	servant

22	LANDLORD			TENANT	
wharf	mortgagee	russian	square	mortgager	report

23	TEETH			CHEW	
heart	gap	valid	tongue	white	pump

24	MONROVIA			VIENNA	
Moscow	Liberia	Rome	Austria	Nice	Tunisia

25	PEN			PAINTBRUSH	
draw	write	ink	paint	wash	brush

26	URBAN			RURAL	
avenue	city	close	centre	crescent	village

27	CHURCH			MOSQUE	
clergy	christianity	feast	islam	harvest	chant

28	DARK			LIGHT	
eclipse	rain	night	moon	day	rays

29	COMMON			FEW	
usual	rare	timely	many	daily	weeks

30	STORY			TELL	
song	melody	poem	cross	recite	pace

31	HAMMER			ANVIL	
chorus	pestle	marble	mortar	round	long

32	POTTERY			SHARD	
hot	bone	shape	fragment	platform	break

33	SHEEP			BLEAT	
cow	mice	dog	fly	bark	miaow

34	SCHOOL			CHILDREN	
university	tutorial	present	club	clever	students

35	CINEMA			AUDIENCE	
film	documentary	match	crowd	ladies	uniform

36	BOY		MASCULINE		
lass	chance	borrow	feminine	man	house

37	KETTLE		BOIL		
hot	water	oven	bake	spicy	tasty

38	HEADTEACHER		DEAN		
europe	leader	school	dormitory	residence	university

39	GO		DEPART		
come	lounge	reserve	arrive	book	await

40	DICTIONARY		SONG		
words	poise	basket	slant	lyric	grain

TEST 5.9 (Answers on page 221)

Find the word that is closest in meaning to the word in capitals. Write your answer in the box. See how many you can do in 9 minutes.

1 BREATHTAKING   **Answer**

A	B	C	D	E
swallow	bye	bowl	beautiful	still

2 BICKER

A	B	C	D	E
right	rule	mend	argue	extra

151

3 AFRAID

A	B	C	D	E
scared	woe	sing	weep	change

4 ACCUSTOMED

A	B	C	D	E
tailor	routine	attire	gown	day

5 BULLY

A	B	C	D	E
ignore	walk	terrorise	reverse	appoint

6 DIFFICULT

A	B	C	D	E
easy	weak	about	complex	excel

7 DORMANT

A	B	C	D	E
modern	asleep	enemy	section	liver

8 DYSFUNCTIONAL

A	B	C	D	E
great	grace	healthy	bestow	flawed

9 FABLE

A	B	C	D	E
long	yarn	escort	cut	enquiry

10 EQUAL

A	B	C	D	E
belt	fingers	together	unbiased	whisper

11 BENT

A	B	C	D	E
cult	open	warped	about	squared

12 EXIT

A	B	C	D	E
squire	hostel	come	quit	late

13 HONOUR

A	B	C	D	E
window	acclaim	opportunity	mastery	belt

14 HANDLE

A	B	C	D	E
monarch	festive	domain	manage	locate

15 ADMIT

A	B	C	D	E
adore	confess	adorn	manipulate	guess

16 DECREASE

A	B	C	D	E
elude	attack	growth	diminish	grand

17 CERTIFY

A	B	C	D	E
accredit	score	squire	affect	mean

18 DOOMED

A	B	C	D	E
condemned	involve	endure	dislocate	entice

19 EERIE

A	B	C	D	E
worn	wasp	uncanny	enjoy	lingered

20 DULL

A	B	C	D	E
bright	colourful	shiny	drab	shape

21 DEFEND

A	B	C	D	E
hair	safeguard	length	shower	acquire

22 FAZE

A	B	C	D	E
embarrass	table	slim	lemon	garden

23 FLEE

A	B	C	D	E
revolve	allocate	pantry	balcony	retreat

24 EARMARK

A	B	C	D	E
bell	label	willow	telephone	transmit

In some situations test publishers such as SHL, will include different types of verbal reasoning tests in one test. Test 5.10 illustrates this. Attempt doing the test.

TEST 5.10 (SHL PRACTICE TEST)

(Answers on page 221)

For each question, choose the correct answer from the five possible answers. See how many you can do in 3 minutes.

1 All employees should ...... from such a training scheme.   **Answer**

A	B	C	D	E
result	credit	succeed	enrol	benefit

2 Hard is to soft as hot is to ......

A	B	C	D	E
cool	warm	cold	icy	tepid

3 Which of the following words is closest in meaning to toxic?

A	B	C	D	E
putrid	poisonous	bitter	contagious	inedible

4 All exposed pipes will have to be ...... to protect them from freezing.

A	B	C	D	E
insulated	regulated	connected	incorporated	hot

5 Which of the following words is closest in meaning to vertical?

A	B	C	D	E
horizontal	parallel	straight	perpendicular	flat

6 Stay is to leave as advance is to ......   **Answer**

A	B	C	D	E
arrive	exit	retreat	come	hold

7 A straight edge should be used to ensure that the ends of the shelves are correctly ......

A	B	C	D	E
tightened	aligned	concentric	separated	flat

8 Adept means the same as ......

A	B	C	D	E
energetic	inefficient	enthusiastic	awkward	skilful

6 VERBAL SEQUENCE

Verbal sequence tests assess your ability to organise material so that it makes the most sense and has the greatest logical structure. These tests are usually presented in the following ways:

- hidden words;

- mixed sentences;

- sentence sequence.

HIDDEN WORDS

There are many variations to this type of question. It could come in a crossword puzzle format and words may be hidden in initial letters, final letters, middle letters and so on. Daily newspapers have crossword puzzles and the Internet also has useful practice materials.

Examples of words hidden in a sentence are illustrated below.

1 Women cra**ve st**ability in a relationship. The hidden word is VEST.
2 The little gir**l ate** the loaf of bread. The hidden word is LATE.

Hidden word exercises may sometimes be used to test your knowledge of specific themes and subjects such as history, biology, maths and catering, to name a few. In some exercises a word may sometimes be hidden in a sentence along with the description of the word. For example: This roman emperor enjoyed a **fine ro**mance. The hidden word is NERO. The two sentences below are sample tests focusing on specific subjects. You are expected to find the hidden words related to the specific subjects mentioned.

1   **Catering:** George passe**s a lad** named Michael on the factory floor. The hidden word here is SALAD.
2   **Mathematics:** The ver**min us**es magic to impress people. The hidden word here is MINUS.

There are so many variations to hidden word tests, but do not worry because the objective is always the same. You will, of course, have to be prepared and the test organisers may provide you with sample materials.

MIXED SENTENCES

In mixed sentence tests you are provided with sentences in which the position of two words in each sentence has been swapped so that the sentences no longer make sense. Your task is to read the sentences carefully, identify the two words and underline the words. The example below will help you understand when presented with such questions.

SAMPLE TEST

Ms Campbell has elderly but dislikes being with groups of retired people.

The sentence should read: Ms Campbell has retired but dislikes being with groups of elderly people. So the two words that should be underlined are: <u>elderly</u> and <u>retired</u>.

SENTENCE SEQUENCE

The objective here is to test how quickly you can make sense of sentences, so the time allocation is usually limited. You will be presented with a number of passages of prose, each consisting of three to four sentences, in which the original order of the sentences has been changed. Read through the sentences in each question to get the sense of the passage, and then decide the correct sequence of the sentences. Use the letters or number at the front of the sentences to record the correct sequence on the answer sheet. Complete the first column of the answer box to record the letter or number of your selected first sentence, the second column to record your selected second sentence and so on.

EXAMPLE

A When the British Government imposed a stamp tax and later a tea tax on the colonists, they were bitterly opposed, and measures of repression provoked the colonists to arm. **B** The struggle originated in the resentment of the colonists against such measures as the Navigation Acts, which subordinated America to British commercial and industrial interests. **C** The war of American Independence involved a revolt of the British colonies in North America and resulted in the establishment of the USA. **D** The first shots were fired at Lexington where troops, sent to seize these illegal military stores, were attacked by the militia.

Answer

The answer is **CBAD,** which is recorded on the answer sheet like this:

	1st	2nd	3rd	4th
A			▨	
B		▨		
C	▨			
D				▨

Explanation

The sense of the passage covers events leading up to the outbreak of the American War of Independence.

D comes after **A** – 'military stores' in **D** refers to 'arm' in **A**.

A comes after **B** – The 'measures of repression' in **A** refers to 'such measures' in **B**.

B comes after **C** – 'The struggle' in **B** refers to the 'war' in **C**.

Now try the following hidden words, mixed sentences and sentence sequence questions.

TEST 6.1 *(Answers on page 222)*

In these sentences a word is hidden at the end of one word and the beginning of the next word. Your task is to find the pair of words that contains the hidden word. Write the answer down on the dotted line. See how many you can do in 6 minutes.

1 The young girl ate the curry. ....

2 Dave raged on about the broken relationship. ....

3 The sports car belongs to him. ....

4 Tom will be home at seven o'clock. ....

5 Sabina feels low because of her health. ....

6 Esther, send the children to bed for me. ....

7 Chloe painted the door with emulsion paint. ....

8 Why didn't Tim escort her back? ....

9 This carpet needs cleaning. ....

10 I agree not to misbehave at the party. ....

11 Lydia met Luke in church. ....

12 Ask the registrar if you can pay the fee later. ....

13 He made skiing look very easy. ....

14 She saw that all the food was sweetened. ....

15 You can only admire him. ....

16 Don met Richard Pope for lunch yesterday. ....

There now follows two mixed sentences tests with a time allocation of 15 minutes each. See how many you can do in the allocated time. Underline the answers in pencil so that you can do them again should you want to.

TEST 6.2 *(Answers on page 222)*

Time: 15 minutes

1 Comfortable in our relax chairs and enjoy our excellent hot beverages or cooling fruit juices.

2 It is Robert's hour lunch and he would like a glass of orange juice and a sandwich.

3 My experience personal as a parent is that I have to be organised and decide to choose my battles wisely.

4 One of the good things about being on holiday is that there are many useful booklets that make information to enable tourists to provide decisions as to which historic sites to visit.

5 A good recruitment to the alternative test is used by your company.

6 The borough is creating more spaces open with picnic areas for families with young children.

7 Restaurant candle-lit friendly serving traditional French and Italian meals.

8 Please leave the sky grey of England behind you and come and visit us in the South of France.

9 The children always finished playing around before we've start.

10 During our holiday we did not stay in a youth hotel but in an expensive hostel.

11 Camping is seen as many young people and families by a cheap way of understanding nature and meeting new people.

12 There are three different charge – one star, two star and three star, so you pay an overnight grades according to the hotel you stay in.

13 It is a regret of much matter to the family that his athletic career has been cut short in such a dramatic manner.

14 In the important run, what she said may not be as long as it is today.

15 There is a new musical life about the play of the well-known actor and singer.

16 For many school people sport is an important part of young life.

17 If someone is in a practise, it means a lot of extra team and often spending weekends away.

18 This regional park is part of the Wembley Valley water park.

19 The Sunday club meets at weekends, usually on a nature afternoon.

20 The local variety sports centre offers a community of activities – snooker, indoor football, badminton and karate.

TEST 6.3 *(Answers on page 223)*

See how many you can do in 15 minutes. Underline the two words.

1 The built theatre in Regent Street was adventure for young artists.

2 Steve is 24 and he has been thinking of taking up sport as a sailing.

3 Efu Otubushin wants daughter to look after her young someone for three hours twice a week while she goes to flower arranging classes.

4 Larry and his sister are full of energy and they love outdoors and want to be animals every morning but their parents are too busy to go with them.

5 The working farm is for animal lovers who want to learn about this city farm in the heart of the city.

6 Professional expert can provide staff advice and design fitness plans to meet your needs and offer friendly encouragement.

7 You are currently looking as registered for work with Aces Associates but we have not heard from you in a while.

8 The qualified are staff to give advice and teach students negotiation skills.

9 My two main reading are interests and playing tennis.

10 In many government money for training is available from the countries for the very best young sportsmen and women.

11 All doctors agree that over time damaged may be organs by smoking and reckless drinking.

12 There are no magazines of the copies left to put in the bags of the visitors to the exhibition.

13 At one time desert living in the people were said to have lived on camel milk and dates alone for months on end.

14 There has been a newspapers in the world of revolution.

15 There are many TV programmes in which reality and beautiful people lead exciting lives but rich isn't like this for most of us.

16 Sylvester had no money account, no bank invested anywhere but notes were found in various cupboards and compartments in his town house.

17 It took clear over two weeks to police the building and protect the structure before the insurance company decided to renovate it.

18 Kylie doesn't goes which university she mind to as long as there are interesting people and plenty of recreational activities.

19 We provide everything you need to take lighting photographs, whatever the perfect conditions.

20 The best thing to do is to keep at home and stay warm so that you do not give your cold to other people.

TEST 6.4 SENTENCE SEQUENCE (CIVIL SERVICE FAST STREAM SERIES)

(Answers on pages 223–224)

You should allow yourself approximately 4 minutes to complete these questions.

Question 1

A It merely said: 'On no account do nothing.' **B** We have made a number of recommendations in ours, but the final one was most succinct. **C** Yet for the past 10 years that is precisely what has happened. **D** There are two kinds of report; one to cause change, and the other to prevent it.

	1st	2nd	3rd	4th
A				
B				
C				
D				

Question 2

A In 1992 and 1993, it averaged 13 per cent, according to IMF figures, and in 1994 is expected to 'slow down' to 9 per cent. **B** Since the late 1970s, when China's leaders started moving away from the socialist management of the previous 30 years, the economy has been the strongest performing in the world. **C** If it grows at a similar pace for the next 25 years, China would become the biggest economy in the world. **D** Since 1980, it has grown by more than 9 per cent a year.

	1st	2nd	3rd	4th
A				
B				
C				
D				

Question 3

A Only in the 1940s and 1950s, when London's pea-souper smogs started to kill thousands of people, was any action taken. **B** Apart from the occasional irritation of woodsmoke in poorly ventilated buildings, people could take the air they breathed for granted. **C** Over the centuries, humankind has shown a marked disregard for the fragile atmosphere that makes life on this planet viable. **D** Prior to the industrial revolution, such disregard was not unreasonable.

	1st	2nd	3rd	4th
A				
B				
C				
D				

Question 4

A Both are essential to the success of the operation but standardisation must take priority at this time. **B** It is necessary to persuade the various divisions that the standardisation in procedure and equipment is necessary. **C** A commitment from divisions to the idea of communication with external agencies is also important. **D** In the final analysis, the section has two major tasks.

	1st	2nd	3rd	4th
A				
B				
C				
D				

7 VERBAL EVALUATION

Verbal evaluation tests are commonly referred to as critical reasoning tests. They are generally mini reading-comprehension exercises. These questions are meant to test your understanding of meaning, implication and structure of passages. The passages are usually followed by four or five questions. Your task is to evaluate each statement given the information or opinions contained in the passage, and to tick the appropriate box in the answer section. You will then be required to decide which statement is 'true', 'false' or 'cannot tell'. For a statement to qualify as TRUE, it should follow logically from statements in the passage or it should be a conclusion in the passage that cannot be challenged. A statement will qualify as FALSE if it does not follow logically from the statements in the passage or a conclusion that from the information provided in the passage can be challenged. To qualify as CANNOT TELL, there should be insufficient information in the passage that makes it difficult to decide if the statement is true or false. Remember to only rely on the information provided in the passage and not on your real life experiences.

The passages can be about any aspect of life such as business, science, social science and faith so it is important to be well equipped. It is difficult to know the topic that will be examined, as there is a vast range of topics to choose from. You can, however, improve your general knowledge by reading the newspapers, professional and trade journals, listening to the news, taking up a hobby, the list is endless but whatever constructive step you take will contribute to enhancing your knowledge. Verbal evaluation questions are quite popular with companies. Attempt the SHL tests below and see how well you do.

TEST 7.1 (SHL PRACTICE TEST)

(Answers on pages 225–226)

In this test you are required to evaluate each statement in the light of the passage preceding it. Read through the passage and evaluate the statements according to the rules below.

Tick Box A   If the statement is true given the information in the passage.

Tick Box B   If the statement is false given the information in the passage.

Tick Box C   If you cannot say whether the statement is true or false without further information.

See how many you can answer in 5 minutes.

> The cafeteria is open at 7 a.m. Lunch is served between 11.30 a.m. and 2.30 p.m. If you require a meal after 2.30 p.m. you must tell the chef before 2 p.m. Guests may be brought into the cafeteria if a special pass has been obtained from the catering manager.

                                                                                      A   B   C

1   The cafeteria is open at breakfast time.

2   You can have lunch at 1.30 p.m. if you wish.

3   If you want a meal after 2.30 p.m., you must inform the catering manager.

4   The cafeteria is strictly for members of staff only.

All clerical staff should use form FPM2 to annually renew their security pass unless they wish to change any personal details. In this case, they should use either form FPM1 or FPM3. Form FPM1 should be used when staff members have been promoted, whereas form FPM3 should be used if other personal details have been changed, eg, address, department etc. Lost security passes must be replaced using form GPM2. The supervisor will supply this form when he/she is informed of the loss of the pass.

A B C

5 Mrs Jeffrey has lost her security pass. She should fill in form GPM2 to obtain a new one.

6 Form FPM3 should not be used to renew a security pass following a promotion.

7 Mr McCarthy has changed his address within the last twelve months. He should fill in form FPM2.

8 Staff must pay to have lost security passes replaced.

TEST 7.2 (SHL PRACTICE TEST)

(Answers on pages 226–227)

In this test you are given two passages, each of which is followed by three statements. Your task is to evaluate the statements in the light of the information or opinion contained in the passage and to select your answer according to the rules given below. See how many you can answer in 4 minutes.

Tick Box A

True: the statement follows logically from the information or opinions contained in the passage.

Tick Box B

False: the statement is obviously false from the information or opinions contained in the passage.

Tick Box C

You **cannot say** whether the statement is true or false without further information.

The big economic difference between nuclear and fossil-fuelled power stations is that nuclear reactors are more expensive to build and decommission, but cheaper to run. So, disputes over the relative efficiency of the two systems revolve not just around the prices of coal and uranium today and tomorrow, but also around the way in which future income should be compared with current income.

A B C

1 The main difference between nuclear and fossil-fuelled power stations is an economic one.

A B C

2 The price of coal is not relevant to discussions about the relative efficiency of nuclear reactors.

3 If nuclear reactors were cheaper to build and decommission than fossil-fuelled power stations, they would definitely have the economic advantage.

At any given moment we are being bombarded by physical and psychological stimuli competing for our attention. Although our eyes are capable of handling more than 5 million bits of data per second, our brains are capable of interpreting only about 500 bits per second. With similar disparities between each of the other senses and the brain, it is easy to see that we must select the visual, auditory, or tactile stimuli that we wish to compute at any specific time.

A B C

4 Physical stimuli usually win in the competition for our attention.

5 The capacity of the human brain is sufficient to interpret nearly all the stimuli the senses can register under optimum conditions.

6 Eyes are able to cope with a greater input of information than ears.

TEST 7.3 (SHL PRACTICE TEST)

(Answers on pages 227–228)

In this test you are given two passages, each of which is followed by three statements. Your task is to evaluate the statements in the light of the information or opinion contained in the passage and to select your answer according to the rules given below. See how many you can answer in 4 minutes.

Tick Box A	**Tick Box B**	**Tick Box C**
True: the statement follows logically from the information or opinions contained in the passage.	**False:** the statement is obviously false from the information or opinions contained in the passage.	You **cannot say** whether the statement is true or false without further information.

Among the useful features available on this computer system is the Notebk feature. The Notebk feature organises lists of information in a record format. Its most obvious use is for lists of names, phone numbers and addresses but many other applications can be defined. One of the biggest advantages of using Notebk is that the files are stored in a format that can be used directly by other features. This means that files do not have to be converted or altered in any way.

A B C

1 The Notebk feature can only be used to organise lists of names, phone numbers and addresses.

2 If users wish to use Notebk files with other features, they do not need to alter the files.

3 The Notebk feature enables the user to instantly update lists of names and addresses.

Software engineering is an approach to the improvement of system productivity. In most circumstances, it has a modest impact on the productivity of the system during the initial development stage. However, systems developed using software engineering techniques have substantially lower maintenance costs and higher reliability.

A B C

4 Lower maintenance costs can be expected if the system used was developed using software engineering techniques.

5 Systems developed with these techniques are more likely to break down.

6 Software engineering is a widely used methodology when developing new systems.

TEST 7.4 (SHL PRACTICE TEST)

(Answers on pages 228–229)

In this test you are required to evaluate each statement in the light of the passage. Read through the passage and evaluate the statements according to the rules below. Then mark the appropriate box. See how many you can answer in 5 minutes.

Tick Box A	**Tick Box B**	**Tick Box C**
True: the statement follows logically from the information or opinions contained in the passage.	**False:** the statement is obviously false from the information or opinions contained in the passage.	You **cannot say** whether the statement is true or false without further information.

Many organisations find it beneficial to employ students during the summer. Permanent staff often wish to take their own holidays over this period. Furthermore, it is not uncommon for companies to experience peak workloads in the summer and so require extra staff. Summer employment also attracts students who may return as well qualified recruits to an organisation when they have completed their education. Ensuring that the students learn as much as possible about the organisation encourages their interest in working on a permanent basis. Organisations pay students on a fixed rate without the usual entitlement to paid holidays or sick leave.

A B C

1 It is possible that permanent staff who are on holiday can have their work carried out by students.

2 Students in summer employment are given the same paid holiday benefit as permanent staff.

3 Students are subject to the organisation's standard disciplinary and grievance procedures.

4 Some companies have more work to do in summer when students are available for vacation work.

Most banks and building societies adopt a 'no-smoking' policy in customer areas in their branches. Plaques and stickers are displayed in these areas to draw attention to this policy. The notices are worded in a 'customer friendly' manner, though a few customers may feel their personal freedom of choice is being infringed. If a customer does ignore a notice, staff are tolerant and avoid making a great issue of the situation. In fact, the majority of customers now expect a 'no smoking' policy in premises of this kind. After all, such a policy improves the pleasantness of the customer facilities and also lessens fire risk.

A B C

5 'No-smoking' policies have mainly been introduced in response to customer demand.

6 All banks and building societies now have a 'no-smoking' policy.

7 There is no conflict of interest between a 'no-smoking' policy and personal freedom of choice for all.

8 A 'no-smoking' policy is in line with most customers' expectations in banks and building societies.

CHAPTER 3
ANSWERS TO AND
EXPLANATIONS OF TIMED TESTS

For the majority of the questions in the book it is only possible to get them either right or wrong so there is no need for any explanation. This chapter will provide explanations to the questions in Test 6.4 (sentence sequence) and Tests 7.1–7.4 (verbal evaluation).

1 VOCABULARY

TEST 1.1

1	**A**	association	**11**	**B**	demonstrative
2	**A**	archaeology	**12**	**D**	dedication
3	**B**	consolidation	**13**	**B**	extravaganza
4	**C**	bankruptcy	**14**	**A**	cordial
5	**A**	comprehensive	**15**	**B**	consecutive
6	**A**	almanac	**16**	**C**	photography
7	**B**	astronaut	**17**	**A**	demineralize
8	**D**	butcher	**18**	**B**	hippopotamus
9	**A**	concurrent	**19**	**D**	decorous
10	**B**	credibility	**20**	**B**	community

21 **C** cassette
22 **C** efficiency
23 **B** weird
24 **B** degradable
25 **B** coquettish
26 **A** pheasant
27 **A** meteorite
28 **A** interweaving
29 **A** encyclopedia
30 **A** demography

31 **D** alligator
32 **D** pathetic
33 **D** quibble
34 **A** rationale
35 **B** veterinarian
36 **B** preference
37 **A** equation
38 **A** dishonourable
39 **A** relapse
40 **D** horoscopes

TEST 1.2

1 **C** disappearance
2 **B** programmer
3 **D** inconvenience
4 **B** entertainment
5 **B** integers
6 **B** grouse
7 **C** representative
8 **D** influence
9 **A** enthologue
10 **C** forensics
11 **B** paradigm

12 **D** naturalist
13 **B** pursuit
14 **C** guarantee
15 **D** predestined
16 **A** nourished
17 **B** curiosity
18 **A** arguments
19 **C** illusive
20 **D** bizarre
21 **A** ointment
22 **A** scandal

23 **C** fragrance

24 **C** modification

25 **B** mystery

26 **C** listener

27 **A** adage

28 **B** confrontation

29 **B** morose

30 **D** haunt

31 **D** derision

32 **D** frivolous

33 **D** route

34 **A** impatient

35 **B** paraphrase

36 **C** flattery

37 **A** anonymous

38 **C** hypnotise

39 **C** deliberately

40 **A** arrogant

TEST 1.3

1 **B** consistency

2 **B** bitterness

3 **A** materialism

4 **D** dentistry

5 **D** executive

6 **D** cabinet

7 **C** insecurity

8 **B** influenza

9 **C** necessary

10 **A** tomorrow

11 **B** pledge

12 **B** discipline

13 **B** eloquence

14 **B** dilemma

15 **B** inspectorate

16 **B** prominent

17 **B** announcement

18 **A** commission

19 **D** scene

20 **D** intervention

21 **B** consultation

22 **C** proposal

23 **A** transparency

24 **D** obsolete

25 **B** strategy

26 **A** chancellor

27 **C** accessibility

28 **C** philanthropist

29 **A** emphasis

30 **C** illuminate

31 **A** familiarity

32 **B** environment

33 **B** rebellion

34 **D** phenomenon

35 **A** accelerating

36 **C** anticlimax

37 **A** caribbean

38 **B** obsession

39 **B** apocryphal

40 **A** affluence

TEST 1.4

1 **D** mercenaries

2 **C** hispanic

3 **B** happening

4 **A** appraisal

5 **A** performance

6 **C** consumer

7 **B** portfolio

8 **A** shareholder

9 **D** directorship

10 **B** battery

11 **C** incinerate

12 **C** compulsory

13 **C** occupation

14 **D** therapy

15 **A** hierarchy

16 **B** corridor

17 **B** asparagus

18 **C** weaning

19 **D** trouser

20 **A** uniform

21 **C** article

22 **B** paradox

23 **A** legitimate

24 **C** superficial

25 **D** rehabilitate

26 **D** fiscal

27 D staggering	**34 C** eccentric
28 D suicide	**35 C** idylic
29 D advertising	**36 A** equity
30 B grotesque	**37 A** dignitaries
31 B extricate	**38 D** painstakingly
32 C gridlock	**39 A** prestige
33 C wharf	**40 C** bureaucracy

TEST 1.5

	Incorrect	**Correct**
1 C	curryculum	curriculum
2 C	afixis	affixes
3 A	albatrose	albatross
4 A	arears	arrears
5 B	bouming	booming
6 C	deeplete	deplete
7 B	detailled	detailed
8 A	desociate	dissociate
9 B	eanestness	earnestness
10 D	perversse	perverse
11 D	seieve	sieve
12 A	puzzel	puzzle
13 C	porkcupine	porcupine

14	A	prejudece	prejudice
15	D	iridorlogist	iridologist
16	D	inflamation	inflammation
17	A	therapiste	therapist
18	B	miscelaneous	miscellaneous
19	B	calender	calendar
20	A	intenssive	intensive
21	C	despensary	dispensary
22	C	viadoct	viaduct
23	C	intermedeate	intermediate
24	A	bungalowe	bungalow
25	A	mediume	medium
26	A	milennium	millennium
27	D	grueling	gruelling
28	A	equiped	equipped
29	C	annoyarnces	annoyances
30	D	routin	routine
31	A	aliances	alliances
32	B	pesimistic	pessimistic
33	B	profesor	professor
34	B	bordensome	burdensome
35	D	suficiente	sufficient

		Incorrect	Correct
36	**D**	carbohidrate	carbohydrate
37	**C**	parrasite	parasite
38	**D**	ossteopaty	osteopathy
39	**C**	imigrante	immigrant
40	**A**	parfunctoury	perfunctory

TEST 1.6

		Incorrect	**Correct**
1	**D**	tranquile	tranquil
2	**B**	sorrowgate	surrogate
3	**B**	philosorpher	philosopher
4	**B**	anihilation	annihilation
5	**C**	infalible	infallible
6	**A**	statuetory	statutory
7	**D**	agresive	aggressive
8	**B**	kinddagatten	kindergarten
9	**A**	flabagasted	flabbergasted
10	**A**	aggenda	agenda
11	**D**	cadeovascular	cardiovascular
12	**B**	comonwealth	commonwealth
13	**B**	exagirate	exaggerate
14	**B**	skeptecism	scepticism

15	D	auxelearies	auxiliaries
16	C	experdetion	expedition
17	A	onfastin	unfasten
18	B	parmitte	permit
19	D	greggarious	gregarious
20	B	dicoy	decoy
21	A	dether	dither
22	A	squeze	squeeze
23	B	enrole	enrol
24	D	bewildar	bewilder
25	C	profesionalism	professionalism
26	C	mldiocre	mediocre
27	D	ambasador	ambassador
28	B	enomouse	enormous
29	C	reinvegorate	reinvigorate
30	C	disfunctional	dysfunctional
31	B	embarasing	embarrassing
32	A	ludecrous	ludicrous
33	C	sovreign	sovereign
34	A	asault	assault
35	C	affordeble	affordable
36	C	accustic	acoustic

	Incorrect	Correct
37 **B**	tornedoes	tornadoes
38 **D**	satelite	satellite
39 **D**	transmesion	transmission
40 **C**	imeasurable	immeasurable

TEST 1.7

	Incorrect	**Correct**
1 **A**	raspbery	raspberry
2 **B**	parleamentary	parliamentary
3 **A**	dislexic	dyslexic
4 **A**	porporting	purporting
5 **B**	acrowbatic	acrobatic
6 **A**	chauvenism	chauvinism
7 **D**	discepline	discipline
8 **C**	snipety	snippety
9 **B**	misoginist	misogynist
10 **D**	exercerbated	exacerbated
11 **B**	domeneering	domineering
12 **B**	claustropobic	claustrophobic
13 **C**	swager	swagger
14 **B**	remeniscenes	reminiscences
15 **C**	sufragetes	suffragettes

16	A	nuroscientist	neuroscientist
17	B	cowardiece	cowardice
18	A	pharmaceuticale	pharmaceutical
19	D	alparbetical	alphabetical
20	B	burdgeriger	budgerigar
21	C	squarre	square
22	C	scouter	scooter
23	B	brarket	bracket
24	A	autum	autumn
25	B	structureraly	structurally
26	A	phisical	physical
27	A	cathidrale	cathedral
28	D	auxieliarie	auxiliary
29	C	vigore	vigour
30	D	imiedeacy	immediacy
31	B	vindecate	vindicate
32	C	dexterrus	dexterous
33	A	proflliegate	profligate
34	D	geolorgie	geology
35	C	seegul	seagull
36	A	teliparthy	telepathy
37	B	narpekin	napkin

38	**B**	promescuos	promiscuous
39	**D**	coasse	coarse
40	**A**	serggent	sergeant

TEST 1.8

		Incorrect	**Correct**
1	**A**	astma	asthma
2	**B**	parseword	password
3	**D**	leathar	leather
4	**A**	generalie	generally
5	**D**	atomique	atomic
6	**B**	freend	friend
7	**B**	dervastetion	devastation
8	**A**	rethym	rhythm
9	**A**	surveylance	surveillance
10	**C**	curveacouse	cuvaceous
11	**B**	cholessterole	cholesterol
12	**D**	tradeesionale	traditional
13	**D**	crytcrion	criterion
14	**C**	desque	disc
15	**A**	parsuade	persuade
16	**B**	byologecal	biological

17 **D** abartoire   abbatoir

18 **D** corregeusly   courageously

19 **A** apertitte   appetite

20 **A** carterlogue   catalogue

21 **D** emberded   embedded

22 **A** gerafe   giraffe

23 **D** deesketes   diskettes

24 **C** chronolorgecal   chronological

25 **C** coalesion   coalition

26 **C** orgernism   organism

27 **C** terapiutic   therapeutic

28 **D** aplerance   appliance

29 **D** cigarrettes   cigarettes

30 **B** varlves   valves

31 **C** embroedered   embroidered

32 **C** rienergarse   reenergise

33 **C** jopardarsed   jeopardised

34 **D** elemenate   eliminate

35 **D** burdgetary   budgetary

36 **C** seelarnt   sealant

37 **B** purnctuetion   punctuation

38 **C** riplernish   replenish

39	A	torbines	turbines
40	A	rifferrals	referrals

TEST 1.9

1	A	herbalist	sponsor
2	B	parallel	adjacent
3	A	sophisticated	jacquard
4	C	flourished	diversified
5	C	asylum	mastectomy
6	A	casanova	cartographer
7	B	stunning	sandwich
8	D	technician	champagne
9	D	trapezoid	upholstered
10	C	allergic	artefacts
11	D	watch	tumbler
12	B	leaseholder	truancy
13	D	prosecutor	chemotherapy
14	C	battalion	excellence
15	C	inconvenience	collapse
16	D	procurement	coriander
17	C	feasible	revision
18	A	university	dramatic

19 **B** glamorous   offence

20 **A** tedious   anaemic

TEST 1.10

1	dermography	49
	discendant	53
2	facinate	68
	sorveillance	100
	dimolish	50
3	alluminium	3
4	ambedextrous	6
	neumonia	98
5	hamsterdam	11
	altogerther	2

6	guestimate	75
	fourfeit	71
7	barroness	20
8	ostrogen	96
	biochemistery	25
	jolity	89
	begamy	24
9	legendery	91
	blackcurrent	28
10	commendasion	37

TEST 1.11

1	biotique	29
	bostale	34
2	forestetion	76
3	devine	63
	androide	14
4	aneckdote	15
	binarie	26
	glandula	79

5	glid	80
	bulwalk	37
	cleate	50
6	desafiliate	60
7	accetate	8
8	gurggle	83
	compeir	53
	densemeter	59

9 egregiouse	69	**10** ghuru	85
gurka	84	bijewell	21
daisiewheel	54		

TEST 1.12

| **1 B** | **3 E** | **5 A** | **7 D** |
| **2 A** | **4 A** | **6 B** | **8 E** |

TEST 1.13

1 C	**4 B**	**7 D**	**10 C**
2 A	**5 E**	**8 B**	**11 A**
3 D	**6 A**	**9 E**	**12 C**

TEST 1.14

1 C	**6 D**	**11 C**	**16 C**
2 A	**7 D**	**12 B**	**17 B**
3 D	**8 E**	**13 C**	**18 E**
4 B	**9 C**	**14 B**	**19 B**
5 B	**10 E**	**15 E**	**20 D**

2 VERBAL USAGE

TEST 2.1

1 hiss	15 suck	29 extent
2 bite	16 read	30 boar
3 heard	17 bee	31 fete
4 sight	18 hair	32 wrest
5 four/for	19 walked	33 wring
6 stationery	20 meet	34 oar
7 council	21 coarse/cause	35 pool
8 great	22 bore	36 quay
9 check	23 hear	37 nit
10 aloud	24 off	38 ail
11 flower	25 by/buy	39 navel
12 sit	26 gripe	40 wrap
13 knead	27 too	
14 new	28 son	

TEST 2.2

1 piece	4 sent	7 waste	10 their
2 access	5 dye	8 male	11 popular
3 read	6 due	9 rain	12 dam

13 accent   **16** dairy   **19** brooch   **22** loan

14 peak   **17** waive   **20** affect   **23** mourning

15 caught   **18** right   **21** three   **24** break

TEST 2.3

1 worked   **9** great   **17** cheque   **25** boar

2 allowed   **10** flour   **18** bite   **26** red

3 be   **11** cut   **19** of   **27** by

4 hair   **12** his   **20** need   **28** pick

5 knew   **13** council   **21** meat   **29** cheek

6 heard   **14** coarse   **22** sock   **30** deed

7 grip   **15** too   **23** stationary

8 here   **16** seat   **24** site

TEST 2.4

1 historical   **7** spent   **13** birthday   **19** heal

2 beaches   **8** less   **14** discussion   **20** stimulant

3 many   **9** nervous   **15** customs   **21** stimulus

4 friendly   **10** polite   **16** sensitive   **22** treated

5 trip   **11** dependent   **17** sensitive   **23** cured

6 hired   **12** ashamed   **18** sensible   **24** stimulant

TEST 2.5

1	SHOP	× + & %
2	POST	% & × $
3	SOIL	× & @ \
4	SPOT	× % & $
5	PAL	% ? \
6	HOP	+ & %
7	SPIT	× % @ $
8	SLOP	× \ & %
9	TIP	$ @ %
10	HOT	+ & $
11	LAP	\ ? %
12	SALT	× ? \ $
13	LIP	\ @ %
14	HIT	+ @ $
15	PIT	% @ $

16	SAIL	% ? @ \
17	STOP	× $ & %
18	TAIL	$? @ \
19	SOAP	× & ? %
20	SLIP	× \ @ %
21	TOP	$ & %
22	HAT	+ ? $
23	POT	% & $
24	HOST	+ & × $
25	SPOIL	× % & @ \
26	HOIST	+ & @ × $
27	SLIT	× \ @ $
28	HIP	+ @ %
29	SLOT	× \ & $
30	SIP	× @ %

3 VERBAL APPLICATION

TEST 3.1

1 a	pretentious		**13 b**	recommendation
2 a	annoying		**14 a**	encouraged
3 a	applicant		**15 b**	claustrophobia
4 a	paralysis		**16 a**	needn't
5 c	partnership		**17 a**	self-assured
6 d	inevitable		**18 b**	successful
7 c	receivership		**19 c**	perplexed
8 d	accomplished		**20 b**	unenthusiastic
9 b	expressive		**21 b**	utterly
10 a	pelted		**22 c**	achievement
11 c	criticised		**23 d**	happy
12 b	contradiction		**24 c**	photogenic

TEST 3.2

1 b	**7 c**	**13 a**	**19 c**	**25 d**
2 c	**8 a**	**14 d**	**20 b**	**26 a**
3 b	**9 d**	**15 c**	**21 b**	**27 a**
4 d	**10 c**	**16 b**	**22 a**	**28 b**
5 a	**11 b**	**17 c**	**23 a**	**29 c**
6 c	**12 d**	**18 a**	**24 c**	**30 d**

TEST 3.3

1 d	6 d	11 d	16 d	21 d
2 d	7 a	12 a	17 b	22 b
3 c	8 c	13 b	18 c	23 a
4 c	9 b	14 b	19 d	24 b
5 b	10 a	15 c	20 b	

TEST 3.4

1 a	7 b	13 b	19 a	25 b
2 c	8 d	14 a	20 a	26 a
3 d	9 b	15 a	21 c	27 a
4 a	10 a	16 c	22 d	28 b
5 d	11 a	17 c	23 b	29 a
6 a	12 d	18 b	24 a	30 d

TEST 3.5

1 c	7 d	13 b	19 d	25 a
2 d	8 b	14 b	20 b	26 d
3 c	9 c	15 b	21 a	27 d
4 a	10 a	16 b	22 b	28 c
5 b	11 c	17 b	23 b	29 b
6 b	12 d	18 a	24 c	30 b

4 VERBAL DEDUCTION

TEST 4.1

1

claw	fish	lair	long	name

Answer | E | D | C | B | A |

2

demilitarise	entwine	eviction	parody	trouser

Answer | A | C | D | B | E |

3

cost	five	pass	read	work

Answer | D | C | B | A | E |

4

contradictions	excursion	impeccable	parsimonious	turbulent

Answer | D | E | A | C | B |

5

cash	rose	smug	this	trip

Answer | A | C | B | E | D |

6

golf	inarticulate	mundane	sympathise	virus

Answer | E | A | B | C | D |

7

alas	book	nose	over	ride

Answer | A | E | C | B | D |

8

aplomb	concoction	diminutive	notoriety	stapler

Answer | D | C | A | B | E |

9

| born | coin | cold | deal | less |

Answer **C** **A** **B** **E** **D**

10

| enterprise | glint | orchid | shelf | virility |

Answer **B** **C** **E** **D** **A**

11

| belt | foot | hand | shoe | tile |

Answer **D** **C** **B** **A** **E**

12

| cascade | coincide | congestion | militant | miserable |

Answer **A** **C** **E** **B** **D**

13

| angle | mixed | polish | pollute | reporter |

Answer **C** **A** **B** **E** **D**

14

| chip | dark | interpret | musical | remove |

Answer **A** **B** **D** **C** **E**

15

| director | instinct | middle | rank | respect |

Answer **E** **C** **A** **B** **D**

16

| exchange | guide | media | prevent | speculate |

Answer **C** **E** **A** **D** **B**

17

| exact | health | mango | path | sauna |

Answer **E** **A** **D** **C** **B**

18

allow	deign	depth	evolution	truant

Answer | A | D | B | C | E |

19

cordial	cosy	cripple	crisis	croquet

Answer | E | C | D | A | B |

20

bunch	croak	four	fraction	usage

Answer | C | B | D | E | A |

21

equator	frame	hindmost	limestone	opaque

Answer | C | A | B | D | E |

22

clock	committee	enhance	public	remunerate

Answer | A | C | B | E | D |

23

gabion	gait	legal	lever	quango

Answer | B | C | A | E | D |

24

gypsy	harmony	heart	hierarchy	hindrance

Answer | B | E | A | D | C |

TEST 4.2

1 **D** curtain   Curtain has nothing to do with flooring.

2 **D** wood   Is not a drink.

3 **C** coffee   Is a drink.

4	**D** hot	This is not a noun.
5	**D** road	This is not related to leg.
6	**B** curry	Not made with pastry.
7	**D** cough	Not done using the nose.
8	**A** dictate	Not related to posting.
9	**C** pillow	Not a cover.
10	**A** floppy disc	Not part of a computer.
11	**A** period	Not on a clock.
12	**B** spinach	Not a fruit.
13	**C** fibula	Not part of the head.
14	**D** finger	Not jewellery.
15	**C** spray	Not part of a house.
16	**D** restaurant	Not an occasion.
17	**D** volume	Not part of a gadget (e.g. telephone).
18	**C** oven	Does not rely solely on electricity.
19	**D** iron	Not a cooling system.
20	**D** boy	Not a specific description of a member of a family.
21	**A** nail	Cannot be found in the mouth.
22	**D** jaw	Not part of an eye.
23	**D** Chester	Not a capital city.
24	**B** writer	Not necessarily a public speaker.

25	**B**	Islam	Refers to the faith and not the person.
26	**D**	translation	Does not refer to a dictionary specifically.
27	**D**	spring	Does not specifically refer to rain.
28	**C**	bracelet	Not an item of clothing.
29	**C**	badminton	A ball is not used in the game.
30	**B**	wider	Does not describe a vertical direction.
31	**A**	zip	Not a cloth.
32	**B**	artist	Not necessarily a singer.
33	**A**	work	Not a description of a time of rest.
34	**D**	judge	Does not express the essence of an issue.
35	**B**	applaud	Not a description of development.
36	**D**	surgery	Not found in a classroom.
37	**C**	driver	Not found in a restaurant.
38	**B**	acrylic	Not a natural fibre.
39	**D**	garlic	Not green in colour.
40	**D**	spoon	Not used for cutting.

TEST 4.3

1	en	**4**	de	**7**	ox	**10**	en	**13**	ex
2	al	**5**	re	**8**	re	**11**	in	**14**	in
3	en	**6**	no	**9**	de	**12**	re	**15**	be

TEST 4.4

1 air	**5** day	**9** gar	**13** non	**17** dis
2 top	**6** tow	**10** mis	**14** dis	**18** saw
3 dis	**7** law	**11** bee	**15** top	**19** dis
4 non	**8** man	**12** gas	**16** par	**20** bed

TEST 4.5

1 easy	**5** baby	**9** jump	**13** deep	**17** bear
2 aero	**6** anti	**10** back	**14** safe	**18** para
3 sand	**7** free	**11** neck	**15** bare	**19** town
4 open	**8** fire	**12** over	**16** over	**20** safe

TEST 4.6

1 table	**4** block	**7** black	**10** green
2 blind	**5** break	**8** multi	**11** tooth
3 press	**6** class	**9** table	**12** blood

TEST 4.7

1 c up	clove	**6 k** it	kin
2 h all	hat	**7 p** ride	pore
3 g ape	gone	**8 t** art	table
4 c harm	coil	**9 l** pace	lace
5 w hen	warm	**10 p** eel	pat

11 p ear	pink	**16 f** rank	flow
12 b ox	bore	**17 p** inch	pore
13 t ape	tall	**18 g** lass	globe
14 s hoe	slap	**19 p** robe	pact
15 b end	band	**20 c** ape	cup

TEST 4.8

1 A make	**7 D** model	**13 D** cause	**19 B** pay
2 E plane	**8 A** tired	**14 B** basic	**20 C** fur
3 A below	**9 C** free	**15 D** strike	**21 B** hay
4 E monk	**10 B** able	**16 E** please	**22 A** nose
5 C worth	**11 E** view	**17 D** tame	**23 D** book
6 A early	**12 C** permit	**18 C** cash	**24 E** deal

TEST 4.9

1 a e i l l r s t w

2 a a e g i i l m n r s

3 a c e e i n r s s t

4 a e g i l l r r u

5 e g l n o o r u y

6 a c i o s t u u

7 e i m o r r r s t

8   a   e   e   i   l   l   s   t   t

9   a   a   c   e   k   n   n   o   r   s   t   u

10 a   a   b   f   l   m   n   o   t   y

11 c   e   e   i   n   o   p   t   x

12 a   i   i   l   l   n   o   r   s   t   t   u

13 c   e   e   e   l   o   p   s   t

14 a   e   e   i   r   s   s   t   v

15 a   e   e   l   m   p   r   x   y

16 a   d   d   e   i   n   v

17 d   d   e   e   e   i   n   n   n   p   t

18 a   e   m   r   s   t   y

19 a   g   h   i   n   n   o   s   t   w

20 a   a   d   e   f   l   m   n   n   t   u

21 c   c   e   f   i   i   i   n   s   t

22 a   a   d   g   g   i   i   l   n   p   r

23 c   c   e   e   e   n   n   o   q   s   u

24 a   a   c   i   l   p   r   t   y

25 a   c   e   e   e   g   m   n   n   o   r   t   u

26 a   b   d   i   i   l   r   t   u   y

27 a   c   c   e   s   s

28 f   i   n   o   s   u

29 c l m o u

30 c g i i l o s s t

31 e e i i l n o s t v

32 a a c d e n v

33 e e e l n o p v

34 a b b i i l o p r t y

35 a c d n o s t w

36 a c e g o r t y

37 a a e e l l n r t t y

38 d d e e e i n n n p t

39 a c e i l n o s t

40 a d f g l n o r y

TEST 4.10

1 generous		**8** keyboard
2 trolley		**9** seldom
3 pancake		**10** expensive
4 lantern		**11** antarctic
5 castle		**12** courage
6 impolite		**13** subtract
7 difficult		**14** envelope

15 parasite

16 broadcast

17 birthday

18 gallop

19 apartment

20 intelligent

TEST 4.11

1 C	6 B	11 D	11 D
2 A	7 C	12 B	17 D
3 C	8 B	13 B	18 A
4 A	9 D	14 D	19 C
5 D	10 B	15 B	20 D

TEST 4.12

1	or	one	11 at	hash
2	hose	tear	12 bank	lace
3	arm	wit	13 tall	sink
4	pan	place	14 not	tear
5	grim	cheap	15 pan	lice
6	bush	trip	16 of	fold
7	on	hotels	17 ear	hat
8	hop	seat	18 all	tact
9	hoe	pant	19 an	ink
10	fee	health	20 lip	flame

TEST 4.13

1 Ev	**6** U7	**11** B10	**16** Ns
2 H8	**7** E20	**12** O66	**17** R12
3 Yb	**8** D52	**13** Ie	**18** I15
4 G	**9** O49	**14** Ke	**19** I43
5 Fa	**10** Th	**15** W85	**20** F2

TEST 4.14

It is sometimes possible for your layout to differ from those given in these answers.

1

g	r	e	e	n
r				e
a				s
n				t
d	o	v	e	s

2

a	b	y	s	s
b				a
o				i
d				n
e	v	e	n	t

3

a	l	i	e	n
l				a
a				s
r				t
m	a	r	r	y

4

p	i	t	c	h
i				o
v				r
o				s
t	e	a	s	e

5

m	o	u	n	t
a				i
r				l
c				e
h	i	r	e	d

6

r	e	l	a	y
i				i
v				e
e				l
t	i	r	e	d

7

t	r	u	s	t
h				a
i				s
e				t
f	l	a	k	e

8

s	c	e	n	t
c				i
o				g
p				e
e	a	g	e	r

9

r	e	a	c	h
e				a
l				s
i				t
c	h	a	s	e

10

f	e	t	u	s
l				c
u				e
k				n
e	v	o	k	e

11

r	o	u	g	h
e				i
l				r
a				e
y	i	e	l	d

12

b	l	a	s	t
l				h
o				e
c				r
k	n	i	f	e

13

m	i	n	e	r
a				i
i				s
z				k
e	n	t	r	y

14

p	i	n	c	h
l				o
a				u
c				s
e	v	a	d	e

15

c	r	o	s	s
l				k
a				a
s				t
s	c	o	r	e

16

s	a	u	n	a
a				p
l				p
a				l
d	i	a	r	y

17

p	o	i	n	t
l				h
u				i
m				g
b	e	a	c	h

18

d	w	a	r	f
u				a
v				i
e				n
t	a	c	i	t

19

d	r	i	f	t
r				r
i				a
n				d
k	n	i	f	e

20

s	t	a	i	r
t				h
e				y
a				m
m	o	v	i	e

TEST 4.15

1 a e e i i l m n r r z

2 c e h m n o o o r s

3 a e e f i l o t x

4 b c g i i l o o o o s y

5 c e e m o s s t y

6 c e h i n n o r s t y

7 a a c e i l m n o r t

8 a c e e l o p r t

9 a e i i n n o o r t t

10 a d e e i m n r s t y

11 a a d g i m p r s

12 c e e g i m n n o o t

13 a e e i i l m m o r z

14 e g i n n n o r r u v

15 a a c e i l p r t t u

16 a a i l o p r s s t t

17 e e i n o p r

18 a b c e i i m n n o o r t

19 a a c d i i i o r t t v y

20 a b e e e i n o r r t

21 a a a d e i l l q r r t u

22 a e i i l n o p r s t u v

23 a c c e f i i i n o r t t

24 a b c d e g h i k l t

25 c d e i i l l m n o s s

26 c c d e i m n o o r s t u

27 a a d d e g i n o r t

28 a e g i l n n o o t

29 a c e e e h m n n n t

30 a a e g s t t w

31 e h l s t t u

32 a c e i m n p t u

33 a a c c d e i i n o r t t

34 a e i i l m n p r r y

35 a a e l l n p p t

36 a c d i i i l l m n p r s t u y

37 a e i o p p r r r t y

38 c e h i n o p r s s

39 e n o o p r r s s y

40 a c e i l n o o p r s s

5 VERBAL ANALOGIES

TEST 5.1

1 **b** transform	21 **b** amassment
2 **a** short	22 **b** unfavourable
3 **b** baseless	23 **b** affluent
4 **b** emblem	24 **b** vindicate
5 **b** huge	25 **b** applaud
6 **a** analogous	26 **c** promise
7 **a** alacrity	27 **a** top
8 **b** agriculture	28 **c** distasteful
9 **c** aggravate	29 **d** playful
10 **c** agenda	30 **b** private
11 **a** gown	31 **b** face
12 **b** carefree	32 **b** affirm
13 **b** bold	33 **b** scare
14 **a** begin	34 **b** concede
15 **c** relieve	35 **a** perform
16 **b** pleasant	36 **a** absorb
17 **b** summerhouse	37 **a** procure
18 **b** aghast	38 **b** optimistic
19 **b** caducity	39 **b** fertile
20 **b** frequently	40 **b** partake

TEST 5.2

1 **C** rapid	9 **D** puncture	17 **C** collect
2 **A** begin	10 **E** dress	18 **C** succeed
3 **B** decrease	11 **B** homely	19 **C** expect
4 **D** sufficient	12 **C** belittle	20 **B** medium
5 **B** error	13 **D** rebellious	21 **A** priceless
6 **E** vital	14 **E** affix	22 **A** tranquil
7 **A** brave	15 **A** cordial	23 **D** negotiate
8 **B** race	16 **A** ground	24 **B** inexpensive

TEST 5.3

1 **c** free	8 **b** impecunious	15 **c** grant
2 **c** concrete	9 **b** devalue	16 **d** embolden
3 **b** approve	10 **a** agitate	17 **d** different
4 **a** nice	11 **a** incompetent	18 **a** exonerate
5 **a** heighten	12 **a** curb	19 **d** inaugurate
6 **a** fix	13 **a** cowardly	20 **b** minuscule
7 **b** nimble	14 **b** help	

TEST 5.4

1 **b** original	3 **c** vertical
2 **b** enter	4 **c** correct

5 **b** relinquishment

6 **b** debit

7 **b** payment

8 **a** contentment

9 **a** ugliness

10 **a** haughtiness

11 **a** untidiness

12 **b** drunk

13 **b** synthetic

14 **a** problem

15 **b** lend

16 **a** cheap

17 **d** pain

18 **c** lament

19 **b** pessimism

20 **d** reward

TEST 5.5

1 **E** laity

2 **A** purchase

3 **B** unlawful

4 **C** obscenity

5 **E** gluttony

6 **A** vice

7 **C** guilt

8 **D** ungenerous

9 **A** like

10 **C** unprivileged

11 **C** misanthropy

12 **B** hatred

13 **D** caution

14 **C** courageous

15 **B** dullness

16 **E** turbulent

17 **D** soft

18 **B** income

19 **C** poverty

20 **A** loss

21 **E** include

22 **A** bondage

23 **D** leniency

24 **E** adversity

TEST 5.6

1 A teacher	9 E spanish	17 B pilot
2 B germany	10 B cake	18 A freight
3 E blows	11 D weak	19 B meat
4 B tenth	12 A scientist	20 A bird
5 A much	13 E poor	21 A chick
6 B team	14 D fingers	22 C mine
7 D find	15 C west	23 B eleventh
8 B read	16 A builder	24 E taste

TEST 5.7

1 d radio	9 c thermometer	17 c bracelet
2 b weight	10 c visa	18 d television
3 c polish	11 b key	19 b baby
4 b wheel	12 c happy	20 b asset
5 c metre	13 b owl	21 b marble
6 c girl	14 b male	22 b hatch
7 b pig	15 c south africa	23 c piglet
8 c actor	16 b dry	24 b soap

TEST 5.8

1 cup   drink   – What things are used for.

2 field   fallow   – The state of things.

3 divide   number   – Make into smaller units.

4 fish   fishbones   – Part of the skeleton.

5 Paris   London   – Countries and their capital cities.

6 debit   credit   – Reverse transactions.

7 mystery   unriddle   – To decode something.

8 minute   seconds   – Different description of time.

9 ship   sea   – Plane flies in the air and a ship sails on the sea.

10 tennis player court   – Actor performs on a stage and the tennis player plays on a court.

11 green   red   – The colour of the vegetables.

12 teacher   lecturer   – Their place of work.

13 beginning   end   – Similar words.

14 cutting   writing   – A knife is used for cutting and a pencil is used for writing.

15 dancer   floor   – Where the person is seen in action.

16 nose   smell   – The functions of these parts of the body.

17 pedestrian   footpath   – A train can be seen on a track and a pedestrian walks along a footpath.

18 legs   motion   – The function of the part of the body.

19 fruit   vegetable   – Apple is a fruit and cabbage is a vegetable.

20 table tennis   bat   – A racket is used to play lawn tennis and a bat is used to play table tennis.

21 master   servant   – Opposite roles and status.

22 mortgagee   mortgager   – Opposite roles and status.

23 heart   pump   – The function of the teeth is to chew and the heart pumps blood around the body.

24 Liberia   Austria   – Monrovia and Vienna are the capital cities of Liberia and Austria respectively.

25 write   paint   – A pen is used for writing and a paintbrush is used for painting.

26	city	village	– Urban refers to city and rural is another word for village.
27	christianity	islam	– The meeting place and the religion practised in it.
28	night	day	– The opposite of dark is light and the opposite of night is day.
29	rare	many	– The opposite of common is few and the opposite of rare is many.
30	poem	recite	– You tell a story and a poem is recited.
31	pestle	mortar	– Part of a whole.
32	bone	fragment	– Part of a whole.
33	dog	bark	– Sound made by animals.
34	university	students	– Place and people.
35	match	crowd	– Place and people.
36	lass	feminine	– Person and alternative description.
37	oven	bake	– Object and what it is used for.
38	school	university	– Leader and institution they work for.

39	come	arrive	– Verb and alternative description.
40	words	lyric	– Dictionary is composed of words and song contains lyrics

TEST 5.9

1 D	**6** D	**11** C	**16** D	**21** B
2 D	**7** B	**12** D	**17** A	**22** A
3 A	**8** E	**13** B	**18** A	**23** E
4 B	**9** B	**14** D	**19** C	**24** B
5 C	**10** D	**15** B	**20** D	

TEST 5.10

1 E	**3** B	**5** D	**7** B
2 C	**4** A	**6** C	**8** E

6 VERBAL SEQUENCE

TEST 6.1

1 Late	**5** Slow	**9** Scar	**13** Desk
2 Average	**6** Rent	**10** Green	**14** Tall
3 Scar	**7** Them	**11** Inch	**15** Anon
4 Meat	**8** Time	**12** Feel	**16** Metric

TEST 6.2

1 comfortable; relax

2 hour; lunch

3 experience; personal

4 make; provide

5 recruitment; alternative

6 spaces; open

7 restaurant; friendly

8 sky; grey

9 finished; start

10 hotel; hostel

11 as; by

12 charge; grades

13 regret; matter

14 important; long

15 life; play

16 school; young

17 practise; team

18 regional; water

19 Sunday; nature

20 variety; community

TEST 6.3

1 built; adventure

2 sport; sailing

3 daughter; someone

4 outdoors; animals

5 working; city

6 expert; staff

7 looking; registered

8 qualified; staff

9 reading; interests

10 government; countries

11 damaged; organs

12 magazines; copies

13 desert; people

14 newspapers; revolution

15 reality; rich

16 money; bank

17 clear; police

18 goes; mind

19 lighting; perfect

20 keep; stay

TEST 6.4

1 The passage is about a report, which has been written, and its lack of impact.

D states the subject of the passage.

B comes after **D** – 'ours' in **B** refers to a 'report', which is introduced in **D**.

A comes after **B** – 'the final one' in **B** refers to a specific recommendation, and **A** states what that recommendation was.

C comes after **A** – 'Yet' in **C** implies a contrast and links what the recommendation was, in **A**, with what actually happened, in **C**.

2 This passage is about the growth of China's economy.

B provides background information to the subject.

D comes after **B** – 1980 is the year that comes after 'the late 1970s' mentioned in **B** and 'it' in me relates to 'economy' mentioned in **B**.

A comes after **D** – 'In 1992 and 1993' is a continuation of the issue mentioned in **D**.

C comes after **A** – 'if it grows' refers to the economy in the previous three sentences. It also seems to be a closing statement and it relates to what could happen in the future.

3 The passage is about air quality over the centuries.

C introduces the subject of the passage.

D comes after **C** – 'such disregard' in **D** refers to 'disregard' in **C**.

B comes after **D** – **B** expands on the sense of **D**.

A comes after **B** – **A** rounds up the passage and follows on, in a time and logical sequence, from the overall sense of **C**, **D** and **B**.

4 The passage refers to a review needed in a business.

B makes the case for the necessity of 'standardisation'.

C comes after **B** – states the other ingredient necessary 'commitment'.

A comes after **C** – confirms that both issues in **B** and **C** are 'essential'.

D comes after **A** – states what is necessary 'in the final analysis'.

7 VERBAL EVALUATION

TEST 7.1

1 The answer is **A**.

This statement is true because traditionally in the UK breakfast is eaten between 7 a.m. and 10 a.m. The passage also states that lunch is served from 11.30 a.m. and breakfast is the first meal of the day.

2 The answer is **A**.

This statement is true because 1.30 p.m. falls between 11.30 a.m. and 2.30 p.m. lunch period.

3 The answer is **B**.

This statement is false because the passage makes it quite clear that the chef must be informed before 2 p.m. The chef and the catering manager are two different people.

4 The answer is **B**.

The statement is false because the passage clearly states that guests can be admitted if a special pass is obtained from the catering manager.

5 The answer is **A**.

This statement is true because the passage clearly states that form GPM2 should be completed if a security pass is lost.

6 The answer is **A**.

The statement is true because only form FPM1 can be used to renew a pass following a promotion.

7 The answer is **B**.

The statement is false because form FPM2 can only be used to renew a pass annually.

8 The answer is **C**.

There is insufficient information in the passage to draw this conclusion.

TEST 7.2

1 The answer is **C**.

From the passage it is impossible to come to this conclusion since 'future income' cannot be accurately compared with 'current income'.

2 The answer is **B**.

The statement is false because the price of coal is very relevant to the discussion.

3 The answer is **A**.

The statement is true because nuclear reactors are currently cheaper to run compared to fossil-fuelled power stations, but the economic drawback is that they cost more to build and decommission.

4 The answer is **C**.

It is difficult to conclude from the information provided in the passage that physical stimuli win over psychological stimuli in the battle for our attention.

5 The answer is **B**.

This statement is false because our brains interpret far less data per second than our eyes.

6 The answer is **C**.

There is insufficient information in the passage to decide whether this is true or false.

TEST 7.3

1 The answer is **B**.

This statement is false because whilst the Notebk feature can organise the lists cited, it is not restricted to these few features.

2 The answer is **A**.

From the information given in the passage, this conclusion cannot be challenged.

3 The answer is **C**.

It is unclear from the passage whether the Notebk feature enables users to instantly update names and addresses.

4 The answer is **A**.

The statement is true since it cannot be challenged given the information presented in the passage.

5 The answer is **B**.

This statement can be challenged since the passage states that systems developed with these techniques are very reliable.

6 The answer is **C**.

There is insufficient information given in the passage to draw this conclusion.

TEST 7.4

1 The answer is **A**.

This statement is true given the information in the passage, which suggests that this is common practice.

2 The answer is **B**.

This statement is false since the passage states that organisations do not give students holiday pay.

3 The answer is **C**.

From the information presented in the passage, it is unclear whether this conclusion can be drawn.

4   The answer is **A**.

This statement is true, since the passage highlights that companies can experience peak workloads during the summer.

5   The answer is **C**.

From the passage it is unclear whether 'no-smoking' policies have been customer driven.

6   The answer is **B**.

This statement is false since the passage clearly refers to 'most banks and building societies' rather than 'all' banks and building societies.

7   The answer is **B**.

This statement is false since the passage clearly states that some customers might be entirely happy with this policy and others sometimes flaunt it.

8   The answer is **A**.

This statement is true. From the information in the passage, the statement cannot be challenged.

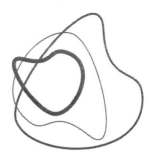

CHAPTER 4
DIAGNOSIS AND FURTHER READING

DIAGNOSIS

Companies use psychometric tests to measure skills that cannot be measured by any other means but are relevant to a job. These tests, as mentioned in Chapter 1, can be used to assess general knowledge or more specific competencies. In the case of verbal reasoning, some of these competencies are spelling, knowledge of the meaning of words, written communication, reading and puzzles. The decision to use a specific test is based on the knowledge required for the vacancy to be filled. In such cases companies generally approach companies specialising in writing and administering psychometric tests to either provide them with the relevant tests or they outsource this part of the recruitment and selection process to them.

The British Psychological Society has developed guidelines to ensure that psychometric tests are used correctly. They expect test administrators to send you a practice test in order to make the test process fair to all. There are also a few Acts of Parliament to prevent unfairness; these are:

The Race Relations Act 1976
The Data Protection Act 1998

The Sex Discrimination Act 1975

The Disability and Discrimination Act 1995

The tests will have to be a good predictor of job performance and be the result of a good job analysis. Verbal reasoning tests have definite right and wrong answers and the results only indicate how well you have performed in the tests. Unlike school, college or university exams, psychometric tests cannot be expressed as a 'pass' or 'fail' on the basis of a single grade. The results can, however, be used as a guide to assist people to identify which of their skills match specific job demands. It is important for you to work within the time specified as this provides you with an idea of how you could perform in a real test environment.

Test results are usually presented in terms of how you have performed in relation to a 'norm group'. The test publishers have a database of scores, which they consider representative of the group they have focused on in their research. The group could be college students, supervisors, graduates, managers or the population in general. This group is referred to as the 'norm group'.

The score on its own does not say much until it is compared with the performance of others. It is worth stating that your score may also depend on how relatively difficult or easy the test is. It is, therefore, important for employers to have the right test for the job. This is the only way that the score can make sense.

In the first paragraph of this book it was said that we are complex in nature, so these tests alone may not show what we are really like, which is why they are a part of the whole recruitment and selection process. They are used to measure skills relevant to jobs that cannot be obtained by other methods. Summarised below is an example of how the scores are interpreted. There are many variables that can affect your performance in the test so your scores may differ. Try to ensure that you give yourself the best opportunity to do your best in the tests.

There are lots of variables to be considered so the test publishers make use of a statistical measurement known as 'normal distribution' to analyse their raw data. Books on statistics will provide you with an in-depth study of this measurement but in this book you will be provided with an insight into the process because it will help you to understand your score. If we suppose you scored 30 out of a maximum of 40 questions, this raw score will be converted into a 'percentile rank'. A percentile rank is the proportion of scores in a distribution that a specific score is greater or equal to. This is to say, that if your score of 30 is equal to or greater than the scores of 85 per cent of the managers and supervisors who have taken the test, then your percentile rank is 85th percentile. You should be provided with information on the reference group or population because it is one thing for your performance to be compared with the population as a whole, and quite another to only be compared with senior managers and consultants. This is because the interpretation would be different.

Mathematicians and statisticians have developed a way of calculating the percentile rank once the 'mean' and 'standard deviation' of a 'normal distribution' are known. Normal distribution refers to the characteristic way in which variables occur in a population and the 'standard deviation' measures how spread out this distribution is. For example, the average height of people in a population is 5 feet 10 inches; this is referred to as the 'mean'. There are people who are shorter and taller than the mean, the spread of these variances is calculated using the 'standard deviation' formula. There are many books in libraries and on the Internet that produce more useful and detailed information. In order for you to know how you did, your score has been set against the general population and Table 5.1 will provide you with an interpretation of your score. The scores in Table 5.1 are just a guideline because it is not possible to compare you (the reader of the book) with a known population. The tests are, however, similar to those that have been tested for reliability, standardisation, and validity so they should give you an idea of how you will perform in the real tests. Do remember that the result is only meaningful if you stick to the time limits. Refer to Table 5.1 to see how you did.

SCORES OVER 85 PERCENTILE (VERY HIGH)

This indicates a very high level of verbal competency and that the person enjoys working with written language. It implies that the person is eloquent and enjoys knowing the correct meaning of words. It also means that the person can accurately communicate information to other people. The person does a lot of reading, possibly solves word puzzles and likes writing.

SCORES BETWEEN 65–85 PERCENTILE (HIGH)

This indicates a very high level of verbal competency and that the person likes working with written language. The person is eloquent and enjoys knowing the correct meaning of words and takes some pride in using them correctly. The person possibly enjoys reading, solving word puzzles and writing.

Table 5.1

			Very low	Low	Average	High	Very high
	Percentile →		Less than 15	Between 15–35	Between 35–65	Between 65–85	Above 85
	Maximum score	Your score					
1 Vocabulary	40		0–12	13–19	20–27	28–32	33–40
	20		0–6	7–9	10–13	14–16	17–20
	10		0–2	3–4	5–6	7–8	9–10
	8		0–1	2–3	4–5	6	7–8
2 Verbal usage	40		0–12	13–19	20–27	28–32	33–40
	24		0–7	8–11	12–15	16–19	20–24
	30		0–9	10–14	15–20	21–25	26–30
3 Verbal application	30		0–9	10–14	15–20	21–25	26–30
	24		0–7	8–11	12–15	16–19	20–24
4 Verbal deduction	40		0–12	13–19	20–27	28–32	33–40
	24		0–7	8–11	12–15	16–19	20–24
	15		0–3	4–7	8–10	11–12	13–15
	12		0–2	3–5	6–8	9	10–12
5 Verbal analogies	40		0–12	13–19	20–27	28–32	33–40
	24		0–7	8–11	12–15	16–19	20–24
	20		0–6	7–9	10–13	14–16	17–20
	8		0–1	2–3	4–5	6	7–8
6 Verbal sequence	20		0–6	7–9	10–13	14–16	17–20
	16		0–3	4–7	8–11	12–13	14–16
	4		0	1	2	3	4
7 Verbal evaluation	6		0–1	2	3	4	5–6
	8		0–1	2–3	4–5	6	7–8

SCORES BETWEEN 35–65 PERCENTILE (AVERAGE)

This represents the score of the typical average person. The person understands words and their meaning but the person may not be good at spelling. The person may sometimes misuse words and may not accurately understand the relationship between words. The person is comfortable with reading and communicating in everyday life.

SCORES BETWEEN 15–35 PERCENTILE (LOW)

This person is not very good with words and does not accurately understand the meaning of words. The person is not good at spelling and is not eloquent. The person does not read a lot and prefers to speak than write.

SCORES BELOW 15 PERCENTILE (VERY LOW)

This person does not have a high verbal aptitude. The person prefers to speak than to write, is not good at spelling and is not bothered about using words correctly.

SUGGESTIONS FOR FURTHER IMPROVEMENT

Your inability to express yourself may prove to be a hindrance to career progression, selection or appraisal processes. It is therefore important to devote some time to improving your verbal reasoning skills. There is no rigid rule to improving performance but there are general and practical guidelines that will help you to improve.

Organisations realise that using psychometric testing contributes positively to the public's perception of their brand image so it is becoming a routine part of most applications or assessment processes. The longer an organisation uses psychometric tests the greater the likelihood of it having a good bank of tests. An organisation with good human resource processes would be able to do a lot of analysis to determine how effective its selection processes are and learn from its mistakes. It is therefore important for you to be thoroughly prepared when your career progression depends on passing these tests.

There is a saying that 'knowledge is power' so you should try taking some tests and see how you fare. This book aims to train you to do your best. It offers sets of questions you can do on your own and in your own time. Generally speaking, it may be important to concentrate on tests that are more related to your chosen career. However, all verbal reasoning tests are always relevant because communication is essential to all spheres of work. It is important for you to have a good know-ledge of English language and how to write correctly. It is also important to be well informed about issues such as current affairs, literature and history and to have confidence in your own abilities and be able to talk about them. You have to take stock of your skill, knowledge, interest, motivation, style and experience and consider how relevant they are to the position being applied for and the test you will be taking. It is generally useful to self-assess and quite important if you desire a change in career.

Tips on taking exams are widely available in libraries, bookstores and the Internet. It is advisable to have increased exposure to information by listening to the news, playing word games such as Scrabble, puzzle books, crosswords and participating in pub quizzes. It is also useful to read newspapers, business journals, novels, trade journals and magazine articles. Refer to the dictionary and thesaurus especially if your vocabulary and or spelling are of some concern. Taking the practice tests in this book will help to highlight aspects of verbal reasoning that you can improve on. Try to remember that the more practice you do the more confident and familiar with the nature and structure of verbal reasoning tests you will be. Listed below are some points that will help you improve your performance.

HINTS ON IMPROVING YOUR PERFORMANCE

Decide to work as quickly and accurately as you can. Be calm, concentrate and remember the rules you have been given. Listed below are some specific things you can do to improve your performance in the various types of verbal reasoning tests.

VOCABULARY AND VERBAL USAGE

- Make a list of words you generally spell or use incorrectly in a pocket-size notebook and refer to it frequently (on the bus, train, spell it on a tape and play it to yourself, etc.). Adopt a strategy that works for you.
- Learn the common prefixes, suffixes and roots of words; some samples follow:

Prefix	Meaning	Example
ad-	to, toward	advance
bi-	two	bicycle, binary
com-	together, with	composite

de-	away, from	deter
ex-	out, of	exfoliate
hyper-	over, too much	hyperactive
mal-	bad	maltreat
mis-	wrong	mistake

Suffix	**Meaning**	**Example**
-able, -ible	able to	chewable
-er, -or	one who does	promoter
-fy	to make	beautify
-ness	the quality of	decisiveness
-ship	the condition of, skill of	relationship

Root	**Meaning**	**Example**
arch	to rule	patriarch
chron	time	chronology
graph	writing	telegraph

- Periodically look up words for their meaning and spelling in the dictionary and thesaurus. Make sentences with these words. Write them down in your notebook.
- When you read, train yourself to notice word combinations, tenses and grammar in general because the choices you are given may contain a word in its various tenses.
- If you do not know, go through a process of eliminating the least likely and then guess. Do not leave any unfilled gaps in the exam.

VERBAL APPLICATION

- Read the sentence carefully so that you understand it.
- For sentence completion questions, think of the words you should insert before looking at the choices available.
- Be aware of clue words such as so, for, because and however as they point you towards the best words that complete the sentence.
- Think of an answer before reading all the multiple-choice answers available.
- If you are not sure, use a process of elimination. In most cases there are two blank words to look for and the chances are that you will at least know one of them.
- Improve your word power. Learn as many new words as possible and practise using them regularly. Learn verb tenses and proper use of adverbs, semicolons, etc.

VERBAL DEDUCTION AND VERBAL ANALOGIES

- Determine the relationship between the words. Note the order of the words and make the sentence as specific as possible.
- Remember that words may have a few different meanings. Think of the appropriate meaning (antonyms and synonyms) and look for the corresponding answer.
- Try to answer verbal analogy questions first because they are short. Doing them first will also help boost your

confidence and save you time which you can then spend on the other sections such as the verbal comprehension questions.

- The hints relating to the vocabulary and verbal application sections are also very useful for these types of questions.

VERBAL SEQUENCE

- Read the passage or sentence thoroughly and as you read, note the tone of the passage or sentence.
- Look for the letter, words or sentences that are to be identified or rearranged.

VERBAL EVALUATION

- Read the question before you read the passage, as this will help you understand the content of the passage. This will save time as you will not have to read the entire passage before knowing the answer.
- Remember that time is of the essence.
- You can decide to answer the questions you find easiest first and then go back to the more difficult ones.
- Remember that all the questions generally carry the same mark so do not waste time on any one question, move on.
- You may want to read questions twice but do not confuse yourself.

ON THE DAY

You must plan to arrive at the test centre in a state that is conducive to achieving your best possible score. This means being calm and focused. It is possible that you may feel nervous before the test, but you can help yourself by preparing in advance the practical details that will enable you to do well. Remember, it is unlikely that you are the only person who is feeling nervous; what is important is how you deal with your nerves! The following suggestions may help you to overcome unnecessary test-related anxiety.

1 Know where the test centre is located, and estimate how long it will take you to get there – plan your 'setting off time'. Now plan to leave 45 minutes before your setting off time to allow for travel delays. This way, you can be more or less certain that you will arrive at the test centre in good time. If, for any reason, you think you will miss the start of the session, call the administrator to ask for instructions.

2 Try to get a good night's sleep before the test. This is obvious advice and, realistically, it is not always possible, particularly if you are prone to nerves the night before a test. However, you can take some positive steps to help. Consider taking a hot bath before you go to bed, drinking herbal rather than caffeinated tea, and doing some exercise. Think back to what worked last time you took an exam and try to replicate the scenario.

3 The night before the test, organise everything that you need to take with you. This includes test instructions, directions, your identification, pens, erasers, possibly your calculator (with new batteries in it), reading glasses, and contact lenses.

4 Decide what you are going to wear the night before and have your clothes ready. Be prepared for the test centre to be unusually hot or cold, and dress in layers so that you can regulate the climate yourself. If your test will be preceded or followed by an interview, make sure you dress accordingly for the interview which is likely to be a more formal event than the test itself.

5 Eat breakfast! Even if you usually skip breakfast, you should consider that insufficient sugar levels affect your concentration and that a healthy breakfast might help you to concentrate, especially towards the end of the test when you are likely to be tired.

6 If you know that you have specific or exceptional requirements which will require preparation on the day, be sure to inform the test administrators in advance so that they can assist you as necessary. This may include wheelchair access, the availability of the test in Braille, or a facility for those with hearing difficulties. Similarly, if you are feeling unusually unwell on the day of the test, make sure that the test administrator is aware of it.

7 If, when you read the test instructions, there is something you don't understand, ask for clarification from the administrator. The time given to you to read the instructions may or may not be limited but, within the allowed time, you can usually ask questions. Don't assume that you have understood the instructions if, at first glance, they appear to be similar to the instructions for the practice tests.

8 Don't read through all the questions before you start. This simply wastes time. Start with Question 1 and work swiftly and methodically through each question in order. Unless you are taking a computerised test where the level of difficulty of the next question depends on you correctly answering the previous question (such as the GMAT or GRE), don't waste time on questions that you know require a lot of time. You can return to these questions at the end if you have time left over.

9 After you have taken the test, find out the mechanism for feedback, and approximately the number of days you will have to wait to find out your results. Ask whether there is scope for objective feedback on your performance for your future reference.

10 Celebrate that you have finished.

FURTHER SOURCES OF PRACTICE

In this final section, you will find a list of useful sources for all types of psychometric tests.

BOOKS

Bolles, Richard N., *What Color Is Your Parachute?* Berkeley, CA: Ten Speed Press, 2007.

Carter, P. and K. Russell, *Psychometric Testing: 1000 Ways to Assess Your Personality, Creativity, Intelligence and Lateral Thinking.* Chichester: John Wiley, 2001.

Jackson, Tom, *The Perfect Résumé.* New York: Broadway Books, 2004.

Kourdi, Jeremy, *Succeed at Psychometric Testing: Practice Tests for Verbal Reasoning Advanced*. London: Hodder Education, 2008.

Krannich, Ronald L. and Caryl Rae Krannich, *Network Your Way to Job and Career Success*. Manassa, VA: Impact Publications, 1989.

Rhodes, Peter, *Succeed at Psychometric Testing: Practice Tests for Critical Verbal Reasoning*. London: Hodder Education, 2008.

Rhodes, Peter, *Succeed at Psychometric Testing: Practice Tests for Diagrammatic and Abstract Reasoning*. London: Hodder Education, 2008.

Vanson, Sally, *Succeed at Psychometric Testing: Practice Tests for Data Interpretation*. London: Hodder Education, 2008.

Walmsley, Bernice, *Succeed at Psychometric Testing: Practice Tests for Numerical Reasoning Advanced*. London: Hodder Education, 2008.

Walmsley, Bernice, *Succeed at Psychometric Testing: Practice Tests for Numerical Reasoning Intermediate*. London: Hodder Education, 2008.

Walmsley, Bernice, *Succeed at Psychometric Testing: Practice Tests for the National Police Selection Process*. London: Hodder Education, 2008.

TEST PUBLISHERS AND SUPPLIERS

ASE
Chiswick Centre
414 Chiswick High Road
London W4 5TF
telephone: 0208 996 3337
www.ase-solutions.co.uk

Oxford Psychologists Press
Elsfield Hall
15–17 Elsfield Way
Oxford OX2 8EP
telephone: 01865 404500
www.opp.co.uk

Psytech International Ltd
The Grange
Church Road
Pulloxhill
Bedfordshire MK45 5HE
telephone: 01525 720003
www.psytech.co.uk

SHL
The Pavilion
1 Atwell Place
Thames Ditton
Surrey KT7 0SR
telephone: 0208 398 4170
www.shl.com

The Psychological Corporation
Harcourt Assessment
Halley Court
Jordan Hill
Oxford OX2 8EJ
www.tpc-international.com

The Test Agency Ltd
Burgner House
4630 Kingsgate
Oxford Business Park South
Oxford OX4 2SU
telephone: 01865 402900
www.testagency.com

OTHER USEFUL WEBSITES

Websites are prone to change, but the following are correct at the time of going to press.

www.careerpsychologycentre.com

www.cipd.org.uk

www.deloitte.co.uk/index.asp

www.ets.org

www.freesat1prep.com

www.mensa.org.uk

www.morrisby.co.uk

www.newmonday.co.uk

www.oneclickhr.com

www.pgcareers.com/apply/how/recruitment.asp

www.psychtesting.org.uk

www.psychtests.com

www.publicjobs.gov.ie

www.puzz.com

www.testagency.co.uk

www.tests-direct.com

OTHER USEFUL ORGANISATIONS

American Psychological Association Testing and Assessment –
www.apa.org/science/testing

Association of Recognised English Language Schools (ARELS) –
www.englishuk.com

Australian Psychological Society – www.psychology.org.au

The Best Practice Club – www.bpclub.com

The British Psychological Society – www.bps.org.uk

Canadian Psychological Association – www.cpa.ca

The Chartered Institute of Marketing – www.cim.co.uk

The Chartered Institute of Personnel and Development –
www.cipd.co.uk

The Chartered Management Institute – www.managers.org.uk

Psyconsult – www.psyconsult.co.uk

Singapore Psychological Society –
www.singaporepsychologicalsociety.co.uk

Society for Industrial and Organisational Assessment (South
Africa) (SIOPSA) – www.siposa.org.za